LINKING

ECONOMIC POLICY

AND FOREIGN POLICY

LINKING

ECONOMIC POLICY

AND FOREIGN POLICY

Charles Wolf, Jr.

Foreword by
Newton N. Minow

A RAND Corporation Book

Transaction Publishers
New Brunswick (U.S.A.) and London (U.K.)

Library of Congress Catalog Number: 90-11225
ISBN: 0-88738-399-8
Printed in the United States of America

Library of Congress Cataloging in Publication Data

Wolf, Charles, Jr., 1924–
    Linking economic policy and foreign policy / Charles Wolf, Jr.
      p. cm.
    Includes index.
    ISBN 0-88738-399-8
  1. United States—Economic policy—1981. 2. United States—
Foreign relations—1981-1989. 3. United States—Foreign
relations—1989. 4. Economic history—1971. 5. World politics—
1985-1995. I. Title.
HC106.8.W653 1991
338.973' 009' 048—dc20
                              90-11225
                                 CIP

To Theresa, who read these in draft form,
and disagreed with fewer than half.

Contents

Part II. Economic Issues and Policy

The Domestic Economic Debate

International Dimensions

Tables

Figure

Foreword

Some years ago, Charlie Wolf briefed the Board of Trustees of The RAND Corporation on a subject to which he brought exceptional insight and keen analysis. At lunch that day, I urged Charlie to write an op-ed piece to bring his thoughts to a larger audience. He did—and this led to the remarkable collection of forty-seven essays assembled here. Courageously, Charlie also has looked back unflinchingly at his work to provide a "postaudit" of his accuracy and relevance. It was no surprise to me to see that he was far more often right than wrong.

Op-ed pieces are a relatively new way to communicate policy analysis. With the declining number of newspapers in the nation, thoughtful editors saw the need to open their pages to diverse points of view and to supplement the work of their own columnists and editorial writers. Major publications now offer a wide spectrum of opinions from nonjournalists to enrich policy debate. Public officials regularly pay attention to the op-ed page, and public opinion is influenced by a particularly well-reasoned and persuasive contribution.

Charlie's contributions have special impact because they challenge conventional wisdom. He often demonstrates that much of what is passed as conventional wisdom "is considered wise because it has become conventional." Not so for Charlie's essays. His uncluttered mind goes to the heart of things—exposing hidden assumptions, destroying sloppy thinking, and provoking thoughtful dissent.

I've now served as a RAND Trustee for more than 27 years and have been blessed with admission to the best postgraduate seminar in the world. Readers of this volume can now gain access to that seminar by exposure to one of RAND's best minds, most facile pens, and farthest seeing visions. Although I often tease economists about their preoccupation with what works in theory rather than practice, Charlie is an economist of a different breed: His work gives equal time to both theory and practice. His ideas work, as you will see when you measure his past visions with today's realities. If you want proof, pay special attention to Charlie's *Newsweek* essay of November 2, 1981 (chap. 22), "Why Economists Disagree."

—Newton N. Minow
Chicago, Illinois
August 28, 1990

Preface

The essays collected in this volume are the original versions of forty-seven op-ed pieces published over the past several years in the *Wall Street Journal*, the *Los Angeles Times*, the *New York Times*, the *Washington Post*, and *Newsweek*, as well as one article published in the *Public Interest* and one in the *Washington Times*. Three of the pieces were coauthored with Henry S. Rowen, formerly of the Stanford University Graduate School of Business and currently in the Department of Defense, and one was coauthored with Sarah Holden, who was at the time a graduate student in economics at the University of Michigan. Several of the essays appear in slightly longer versions than the previously published ones. In these cases, the published versions were condensed by parsimonious editors. Upon rereading, I find the longer versions to be generally preferable.

The collection is divided into two parts. Part I deals with foreign policy, and part II with economic issues and policies. Each of these parts is further divided into two sections: "Views of the World" and "The Soviet Union and China" in part I; and "The Domestic Economic Debate" and "International Dimensions" in part II. For the most part, the basis for these separate sections is obvious, but in several instances the decision to place a particular essay in one section or another is arbitrary. For example, the chapters "America's 'Decline': Myth and Reality" (chap. 2), "'Star Wars' and the Economies of Western Europe" (chap. 8), and "Soviet Economic Reform: Obstacles and Solutions" (chap. 20) appear in the foreign policy section although they involve major economic issues as well. Conversely, "Helping Mr. Gorbachev" (chap. 19), "The Missing Chapter in the International Debt Story" (chap. 41), and "The Weaknesses in Japan's Economic Strength" (chap. 44) are included in the economic policy section, yet they have evident foreign policy implications and might have been included in that section instead.

Viewing the forty-seven separate pieces as a whole, I think they convey two broad messages that none of the essays adequately conveys by itself:

- Economic policy and foreign policy are intimately and increasingly intertwined—the foreign policy implications of the Omnibus Trade Act of 1988 and the resulting Strategic Impediments Initiative are two examples, and the effects of severe economic stringencies within the Soviet Union on Mr. Gorbachev's "new thinking" in foreign policy a third.

- The linkages between domestic and international economic issues are growing ever stronger—a reflection of the increasing internationalization of corporate operations and structures, and of capital, technology, and commodity markets. The links between the trade deficit and the budget deficit provide one example, and the relation between U.S. domestic monetary policy, and foreign capital inflows and U.S. trade deficits, provides another.

These linkages sometimes appear within the individual essays, and sometimes they emerge when several of the essays are considered together. Chapter 26, "A Proper Perspective on the Twin Deficits" (which argues that the perennial hand-wringing and dire warnings about the U.S. budget and trade deficits have been excessive and largely unwarranted) is closely related to chap. 32, "A Panglossian View of the Economy," and chap. 36, "The Trade Deficit: Myths and Realities." Both of the latter essays present a considerably more favorable interpretation of the economy's status, performance, and prospects than the conventional views on these matters.

There is also a close relationship between chap. 27, "Public Deficits and Private Savings," and chap. 28, "What Comes After Gramm-Rudman-Hollings?" both of which suggest that the U.S. budget deficit is a less serious matter—indeed, an issue of secondary importance—compared with the U.S. savings rate, and that there is not a very close connection between the two.

In the foreign policy domain, the chapter on "Soviet Economy and U.S. 'Opportunity'" (chap. 15) foreshadows and is further elaborated in chap. 16, "'Guns Versus Butter' in Gorbachev's Reforms," "What Cuts in Soviet Military Spending Can Do for Perestroika" (chap. 17), and "Gorbachev's Peace Dividend" (chap. 18). These chapters, as well as chap. 19, "Helping Mr. Gorbachev," and chap. 20, "Soviet Economic Reform: Obstacles and Solutions," deal with the connections between the internal economic predicament of the Soviet Union on the one hand and the choices that this presents for the Soviet leadership and for the United States in its relations with the Soviets on the other.

Publishing material written over a seven-year period is a risky business, because it makes transparent one's limitations as a soothsayer. Yet the results are gratifying as well as humbling: gratifying because most of what I said then seems to me no less valid now; yet humbling too, because a few of the earlier pieces on the Soviet Union (chap. 14, "Prospects for the Soviet Empire," and chap. 11, "The Underlying Disagreement About How to Deal With the Soviet Union") suffer from the seeming contextual remoteness of the period before Gorbachev, perestroika, and glasnost. Moreover, in the essay on "The Dollar's Impending Climb" (chap. 42), written in September 1987, my expectation of a rise in the dollar's value in the ensuing couple of years proved dead wrong. I hope this error in predicting the impending appreciation of the dollar is compensated by some degree of prescience in forecasting the likely stamina and endurance of the post-1982 growth of the U.S. economy. This general position is described in chap. 30, "Is the Economy Poised or Paralyzed?" and chap. 31, "Reaganomics, Keynesian Economics, and the Current Recovery." These views contrasted sharply with contrary predictions made at the time by many of the often erring, but seldom daunted, economic forecasters. Their vagaries receive attention in chap. 24, "The Hazards of Economic Forecasting," and chap. 25, "Scoring the Economic Forecasters." My anticipation of the "Tokyo stock market crash" in August 1989 (chap. 45, "Clouds Over Japan's Economic Future") preceded that event by seven months.

I believe that most of the essays stand up well to the passage of time. This characterization applies, for example, to chap. 39, "Clearing the Haze Around International Debt," and "The Missing Chapter in the International Debt Story" (chap. 41), and to the more general chapters on "Events That Probably Won't Happen in 1990" (chap. 1), "Third World: Myths and Realities" (chap. 4), and "Why Economists Disagree" (chap. 22). These essays are as germane to the debate about the issues they deal with as they were when written several years ago. On the other hand, the comparative assessment of restructuring in the Soviet Union and China—"Talk in Moscow, Action in Beijing" (chap. 9)—is much less convincing since the blatant and ruthless use of military force in China in June 1989 than when the piece was originally written. The outlook for China's economic reform is more uncertain than it appeared to be in October 1988, despite reiteration by the Chinese leadership of their intention to move forward with market-oriented, "open-economy" policies. Mr. Gorbachev's dramatic public relations efforts make the discussion of "Consensus and Dissensus about the Soviets" (chap. 10) seem a bit anachronistic. However, the outcome of these matters remains quite unclear.

It is useful and enlightening, as well as sobering, to review what one has written over a protracted period. I recommend that all serious scholars, columnists, journalists, and other pundits who write on policy issues should undertake it periodically to see in retrospect where, when, and why they've been right or wrong, relevant or irrelevant.

In accord with this recommendation, I have reviewed and evaluated all of the pieces in this book—except those published in 1990—in the form of brief "postaudits" attached at the end of each chapter to score my own accuracy and relevance. (I've deferred doing this for the 1990 chapters on the grounds that the interval is too short to provide a fair test.) The results of this exercise are predominantly and substantially confirmatory, although perhaps the reader will be less persuaded of this than I am.

In most of the essays, the views I present and the actions and policies I propose conflict with conventional wisdom. This is sometimes a necessary, though surely not a sufficient, condition for making policy improvements, and for a clearer understanding of the issues and choices that such improvements depend on. For example, the several chapters on international debt argue that the foreign indebtedness of the United States has been misestimated by something in the neighborhood of $300 billion, that the real economic burden of Third World debt is already largely behind us, and that the easing and resolution of the Third World debt problem should emphasize repatriation of capital flight rather than new lending. And three concluding essays on Japan (chap. 44, "The Weaknesses in

Japan's Economic Strength"; chap. 45, "Clouds over Japan's Economic Future"; and chap. 46, "How Socialism in Japan May Help Capitalism in the United States") also advance positions—suggested by their titles—at odds with much of what passes for informed opinion.

On foreign policy matters, several of the chapters suggest that Mr. Gorbachev's perestroika in the economic sphere is more rhetoric than reality; that any form of subsidy in Western lending to the Soviet Union has dubious economic as well as political justification; that perestroika's success depends on Soviet price reform, conjoined with fiscal, monetary, and legal reform, irrespective of external assistance; that Japanese acquisition of real estate and other direct investments in the United States is mutually advantageous and should be welcomed rather than feared; and that federal budget deficits are of secondary importance compared with the decline in the aggregate U.S. savings rate during the past decade.

Although some of the essays are slightly more technical than others, all are accessible to intelligent nonspecialists. I hope readers will derive some satisfaction from comparing and testing their own views with mine, as well as with the conventional wisdom that is contested in these essays. There are two types of conventional wisdom. The first is conventional because it is based on genuine wisdom. The second is considered wise because it has become conventional. My disputes are with what seem to me to be the second type.

In readying this manuscript for publication, I have been immeasurably helped by Donna Betancourt. Her assistance has been invaluable: in retrieving final drafts from multiple earlier ones scattered in computer files over several years; rearranging chapters as the book's organizational structure changed; adding my "postaudits"; and putting it all together.

I. Foreign Policy

Views of the World

1

Events That Probably Won't Happen
in 1990

The remarkable events of 1989 reconfirm the wisdom of Sam Goldwyn's maxim: "Never make forecasts—especially about the future!"

No scholar, intelligence specialist, journalist, or other type of expert in the United States or abroad envisaged, a year ago, any appreciable portion of the extraordinary changes that occurred in 1989 in Eastern Europe and China: election of a non-Communist government in Poland; crumbling of the Berlin wall; peaceful ousting of entrenched Communist leaders in East Germany, Czechoslovakia, Bulgaria, and Hungary; violent overthrow of Ceausescu in Romania; and, in a reverse direction, the brutal reassertion of central control by the Communist old guard in China.

This experience forcefully reminds us of the acute limitations of the established experts. It also suggests another valuable lesson: Perhaps thought and attention should be given not just to what seems likely to happen, but to what seems less likely, as well.

For the most part, human affairs are fairly continuous: Tomorrow's events are usually shaped substantially by those of today. But often the most significant events are ones that, before the fact, appear less likely to happen. They represent instead sharp departures from continuity. The year 1989 was dominated by such departures from what had been considered likely.

In this light, and because the inclination to forecast is such a deeply engrained human foible (notwithstanding Sam Goldwyn), it may be

---

A slightly abbreviated version of this essay was published by the Los Angeles Times *under the title "Consider the Unexpected" on January 16, 1990.*

worthwhile to redirect it from a preoccupation with what is expected, toward consideration of what is unexpected.

Specifically, suppose we ask what specific events might occur in 1990 that would be as far removed from what is presently considered likely to occur, as the events of 1989 were from what was considered likely a year ago? Here are eight candidates:

- A sharp and violent suppression in the Soviet Union of ethnic dissidence and separatism in the Baltic states, Byelorussia, the Ukraine, Moldavia, Armenia, or Azerbaijan.

- Mass demonstrations in East Germany demanding removal of Soviet forces, followed by their peaceful withdrawal.

- Same as the preceding scenario, except that in this variant the forces remain and are used to suppress the demonstrations.

- Amendment of the Soviet constitution terminating the Communist party's monopoly of political power and legalizing development of a multiparty system in the Soviet Union.

- Successful democratization efforts in China (along lines of the changes in Eastern Europe in 1989), reversing the Tiananmen Square crackdown of June 1989 and ousting the present old-guard rulers.

- Invasion of Taiwan by forces from the mainland.

- A nuclear conflict in the Middle East or in South Asia.

- Stock market crash in either New York or Tokyo exceeding that of October 1987, and leading to or accompanied by negative real economic growth and high unemployment.

Viewed from the perspective of 1990, all of these scenarios are unlikely. (The order in which they are listed reflects my own judgment of their successively decreasing likelihood of occurrence in

1990.) But none of them is less likely than the actual events that occurred in 1989 appeared to be a year ago!

In any case, devoting more attention to such unlikely events—both favorable and unfavorable—may serve as a prudent reminder of the limitations of what we know (or think we know), and perhaps as a stimulus to increasing our ability to cope with the unexpected when it occurs.

2

America's "Decline":
Myth and Reality

Alarm about the current and impending decline of the U.S. international position has become widespread, even fashionable, in some academic, media, and congressional circles. Sometimes this pessimism is expressed with regret; occasionally, with something approaching retributory glee. While these differing sentiments usually reflect the political predilections of their respective sources, they generally use the same rhetoric: "decline," "relative decline," "imperial overstretch," "loss of competitive edge," "waning of American ascendancy," and so on.

Among the pacesetters of this rhetoric are Yale historian Paul Kennedy, Princeton political scientist Robert Gilpin, New York financier Peter Peterson, Washington publicist Richard Barnet, and numerous columnists and commentators in the news media.

Implicit in the rhetoric of decline is the notion that some things were far "better," "stronger," or "larger" in the past than at present, and than they will be in the future. Hence, the trend is tilting downward—that is, declining. The idea is clear enough, but the facts don't support it.

One of the frequently cited indicators of this putatively negative trend is the U.S. economy's share of the global product "then" and "now." If "then" is considered to be 1950, clearly the trend has been downhill. In 1950, the U.S. GNP was about 45 percent of the global product, but that was a manifestly atypical year. Europe, including

An abbreviated version of this essay was published under the title "America's 'Decline': Illusion and Reality" in the Wall Street Journal *on May 12, 1988.*

both the victor and vanquished countries, was still depleted or devastated from World War II, as were Japan and the Soviet Union.

If a more appropriate and representative base year is used—say, the mid-1960s (or even a pre-World War II year like 1938)—the remarkable fact is that the U.S. economy's share of the global product was about the same then as it is now: about 22 to 24 percent.

Since the mid-1970s, the economies of Japan and the Pacific Rim countries, including China, have grown more rapidly than the U.S. economy. On the other hand, the U.S. GNP has grown more rapidly than that of Western and Eastern Europe, the Soviet Union, and much of the so-called developing world, leaving the overall U.S. share of the global product unchanged.

According to estimates covering the next two decades recently made in a RAND study for the Commission on Integrated Long-Term Strategy, U.S. GNP in 2010—based on conservative assumptions concerning U.S. capital formation, employment growth, and productivity change—will reach about $7.9 trillion in 1986 prices, representing a real annual growth rate of about 2.6 percent. When this is compared with the higher forecasted growth rates of Japan, China, and several of the newly industrialized countries, as well as the lower forecasted growth of Western Europe and the Soviet Union, the U.S. share of the global product is likely to be about the same in the first decade of the 21st century as it currently is. So, according to this very gross indicator, the future probably won't see a U.S. decline at all.

Another favorite image of the mythology of decline is the U.S. as "hegemonic" in the past and, by contrast, as weakened, bloated, "overstretched," and ineffectual in the present.

To be sure, the United States confronts serious problems—the trade and budget deficits are invariably cited (although it's worth noting, in passing, that Japan's central government debt is a larger fraction of its GNP than is that of the United States, while the foreign indebtedness of the U.S. has been grossly overestimated in the official statistics). Moreover, evidence of the limited U.S. ability to affect important international events is abundant: for example, inability of the United States to convince the NATO allies to bear more of the burden of collective security; limited influence on Japan's willingness to open its markets to competitive imports of U.S. commodities and services; repeated failure to achieve peace and stability in the Middle East;

inability to displace or alter the Sandinista regime in Nicaragua; and long-standing failure to persuade the Soviets to reduce their occupation forces in Eastern Europe.

But memories are short. In the past when, according to the current mythology, the United States was "hegemonic," in fact it was no more—and perhaps even less—able to influence events along directions we desired than at present. Recall, for example, that a Marxist-Leninist regime became firmly entrenched 150 miles from the Florida coast at the start of the 1960s; that nuclear weapons were acquired by France (1960), China (1964), and India (1974) despite strong U.S. opposition; that France exited from NATO in 1967; and that South Vietnam was overrun by Communist North Vietnam in 1975.

In contrast to this unimpressive record of U.S. influence in the "hegemonic" past, the extent and effectiveness of U.S. influence in the current period of "decline" has been substantial: for example, in contributing to democratization in El Salvador, the Philippines, Korea, and potentially in Panama; in securing the deployment of intermediate range nuclear weapons in Europe in concert with our NATO allies, and thereby inducing the Soviets to resume negotiations leading to removal of their SS-20 missiles from Europe and Asia; in leading a substantial allied effort to flag and protect commerce in the Persian Gulf; and in helping, by a combination of pressure and diplomacy, to bring about the impending departure of Soviet forces from Afghanistan.

In another domain, that of broad international economic policies and institutions, U.S. influence in the "hegemonic" 1960s and 1970s was unable to forestall or arrest the spread of collectivist, antimarket policies—reflected in expanded government investment, ownership, and regulation, increased tax rates, and so on—in the Third World, as well as in the other two.

By contrast, in the 1980s, during the period of supposed U.S. decline, this trend has been sharply reversed, at least in part by the influence, example, and policies of the United States. In place of the collectivist trend of the 1960s and 1970s, each of the three "worlds" has experienced a dramatic recognition and expansion of the role of market forces, economic incentives, price competition, and the "privatization" of economic activity.

As to the future, since none of us knows, it's safest to acknowledge the merit of Eisenhower's bland truism (à la Yogi Berra) that "the future lies ahead." In the inevitably uncertain future, the principal committed adversary of the United States will probably experience a relative descent, while the Asian countries—whose relations with the United States will probably be more cooperative than adversarial—are likely to experience a relative ascent. To characterize this complex environment of the future as one in which the U.S. position declines is misleading and simplistic.

The rhetoric of decline is wrong because it portrays a past that wasn't, a present that isn't, and a future that probably won't be!

Postaudit

This rebuttal of the "declinist" argument reads about as well in 1990 as when it was written in 1988.

3

Ideology Has More Than One Face

When the term "ideology" (or its cognates "ideologues" or "ideological") appears in the media, the reference typically has two characteristics: it is critical or derisive, and it is applied to the "conservative right" rather than to the "liberal left." On the basis of casual empiricism—simply counting the recent references I've seen— I estimate the odds are five to one that these characteristics will be associated with the reference!

Three recent examples, among many possible ones, illustrate the point:

- From the *New York Times*: "The Reaganites' ideological obsession with Cuba and Nicaragua has blinded the Administration . . . ."

- From the *Los Angeles Times*: "The President and the ideologues who surround him seem blind to these complexities."

- From the *New Yorker* magazine: "[Reagan] is less leashed, less careful about what he says, more combative, more ideological . . . ."

Why, among the range of controversial issues to which the "ideological" label is frequently applied, is the application so heavily concentrated on one side? Why, for example, are intensified efforts to

A slightly abbreviated version of this essay was published under the title "What's Wrong with an Ideology?" in the Washington Post *on June 16, 1985.*

dislodge the Sandinistas and to thwart Cuba considered ideological, while rejection of these efforts is not?

Why, to take another issue, is strong advocacy of the Strategic Defense Initiative often termed ideological, but opposition to it is not?

Why is it ideological to call the Soviet Union "an evil empire," but not ideological to consider it simply a troublesome, troubled, and perhaps paranoid state?

Why is it ideological to favor defense spending over spending on domestic programs, while the reverse preference is not?

Why is "pro-life" ideological, but "pro-choice" not?

To personalize the point, why is it generally accepted that many of the positions espoused by President Reagan are ideological while those favored by Teddy Kennedy or Tip O'Neill are not? Why is the *National Review*'s William Buckley ideological but the *New York Times*' Anthony Lewis is not? Why the Defense Department's Richard Perle but not the State Department's Richard Burt? Why is Pat Buchanan typically cast as an "ideologue" while Stu Eisenstadt never was? And why is the *Wall Street Journal* considered ideological but not the *Washington Post*?

Why, to generalize the point, is the derisive, put-down label applied to one side so frequently but to the other side so rarely?

The simple answer is that the media that employ the label are themselves antagonistic to the positions they apply it to, and sympathetic to the ones they refrain from applying it to. No doubt there is much truth in this, but it's not the whole explanation.

The rest of the explanation lies in the widely accepted assumption that the positions termed ideological actually are more rigid, less willing to compromise, less receptive to evidence that contradicts them, and hence more justifiably subject to criticism and derision than the contrasting, "nonideological" positions.

In fact, this assumption is unwarranted, not because the factual basis for the so-called ideological positions is strong, but because the factual basis for the opposing "liberal left" positions is equally weak.

Consider the issue of trying to cut the federal budget deficit by reducing domestic spending rather than reducing the growth of defense spending. The case for protecting defense spending while concentrating cuts on domestic programs rests on several key premises: the vulnerability of U.S. land-based missile forces to a

Soviet first strike, and the relative invulnerability of Soviet land-based missile forces to the same threat from the United States; the deficiencies of U.S. and NATO conventional capabilities relative to those of the Warsaw Pact; the need to replace a geriatric strategic bomber force with one that is more modern and more capable; and, most important of all, the assertion that, unlike domestic programs, the federal government provides the only means to meet these defense needs.

None of these premises is without merit, although all of them are arguable, except the final one. There is no one else to do the defense job besides the federal government.

On the other hand, the contrary view about cutting defense spending as much or more than domestic spending rests on a different, and opposed, set of key premises: namely, the Soviets are and will remain fully deterred by existing sea-based missile forces; NATO's conventional capabilities are, even if less than desirable, quite adequate compared to those of the Warsaw Pact, partly because the non-Soviet forces in the Pact are too unreliable for the Soviets to be confident of using them; the B-52 bomber force is old, but it can hang on until the stealth replacement arrives; and finally, while it's true that the federal government is the only means of providing for defense, waste should not be protected by this lame excuse, and various domestic programs (for example, social security benefits, student loans, even Amtrak) are important and won't get done unless the federal government does them.

The point of this attempt at constructing a fair balance is simply that the second set of arguments is no less arguable or more convincing than the first. In both cases, corroborative as well as conflicting evidence must be marshaled, compared, evaluated, and in the final analysis, subjected to fallible human judgment to arrive at a personal or a policy conclusion. But most assuredly, the pro-defense view is no more ideological than its opposition.

The same sort of balance sheet, with the same conclusion, can be arrived at for all the other issues mentioned earlier.

When someone impugns the views of another as being ideological, it's usually a safe bet that the comment applies at least equally to the source as to the object.

Postaudit

The essay's general point is no less relevant now than when it was written five years ago. Of course, the examples relating to the defense budget have lost some of their validity in light of the major changes that have occurred in Eastern and Central Europe, the Soviet Union, and the Warsaw Pact.

4

Third World: Myths and Realities

When Alexander M. Haig, Jr., testified before the Senate Foreign Relations Committee on his nomination as Secretary of State, he observed that the Third World ("a misleading term if ever there was one") is a myth. "Recent American foreign policy," Haig said, "has suffered from the misperception which lumps together nations as diverse as Brazil and Libya, Indonesia and South Yemen, Cuba, and Kuwait . . . . [The] failure to tailor policy to the individual circumstances of developing nations has frequently aggravated the very internal stresses which Western policy should seek instead to diminish."

Following Haig's lead, it may be timely to try to separate myths from realities, because the conventional wisdom about the so-called Third World is more conventional than wise.

Myth: The "Third World," consisting of some 130 less-developed nations, is a reasonably cohesive entity, unified by similar interests and ideologies that enable its members to act effectively and in concert.

Reality: The nations of the Third World are in fact divided in many more ways and by many more conflicting interests than those that unify them. Of course, it is a fact that certain attitudes—intense nationalism, hypersensitivity to foreign condescension, and a liking, perhaps waning, for socialist ideology, to name a few—are shared by many developing nations. But more objective circumstances tend to divide them. For example, the Third World includes oil importers (Brazil, India, Pakistan) and oil exporters (Saudi Arabia, Libya, Iraq,

---

A slightly abbreviated version of this essay was published by the Los Angeles Times *on January 27, 1981.*

Mexico, Venezuela); rapidly growing economies (Korea, Brazil, Singapore) and slowly growing or stagnating ones (most of the remaining nations); centrally planned economies as well as market economies; major international debtors (Brazil, Mexico, Turkey) and major international creditors (Saudi Arabia, Libya, Kuwait); communist nations, pro-communist nations, and vigorously anti-communist nations (as well as many in between); and nations ruled by military regimes and nations that profess the primacy of civil over military control.

The rhetoric of Third World unity is more spurious than real. The reality of the Third World is cultural, political, and economic diversity.

Thus, almost any action by the Reagan Administration is likely to evoke support from some Third World nations, opposition from others, and indifference from many. Our policymakers would be well advised to think about the Third World as a plural, not a singular, entity.

Myth: Achieving significant and sustained economic development in the Third World is an overwhelming and intractable problem, made even more difficult by the rigidity and discrimination of the present international economic order.

Reality: Achieving rapid and sustained development, within the current international economic order, is a much less formidable problem than is usually supposed. The means and methods for realizing economic development are well known, have been widely demonstrated, and are generally acknowledged even if they are not widely adopted. By and large, these recipes have been amply demonstrated by the impressive development of the small number of Third World nations (Brazil, Korea, Taiwan, and Singapore) that have maintained average rates of real economic growth of 9 percent annually during the 1970s.

These nations have made economic progress possible by achieving political stability, including infrequent changes of government. In addition, such nations have provided a hospitable economic climate for market forces and market prices, have encouraged infusions of foreign capital and the selective import of foreign technology, and have avoided hyperinflation.

Orientation toward the market, while typical of these relatively successful Third World nations, does not necessarily imply private ownership or an inactive role for government. Where government interventions occur, they usually are selective and limited in number.

As to the rigidity and adverse effects of the present economic international order, and the sometimes shrill call for a "new international economic order," again the reality departs sharply from the myth. In fact, the "old" order has been remarkably flexible, rather than rigid, and hospitable rather than resistant to development in the Third World.

For example, the drastic shift from a regime of fixed exchange rates to fluctuating ones, the recycling of several hundred billion dollars of petrodollars over the last half dozen years, and the transfer of technology, are all indications of the adaptability of the present international economic setup to changing needs and forces.

Myth: Economic development is essential for political stability and democratization in the Third World.

Reality: There is no significant relationship between economic development and either political stability or democratization. Nations such as South Korea developed dramatically while deferring significant progress toward democracy. Nations such as India have maintained relatively democratic and stable institutions without notable success in economic development. In some nations—for example, Iran—rapid economic development has brought with it political instability. And in some nations, such as Turkey, adverse economic conditions have provided an environment in which terrorism has flourished and emerging democratic institutions have been set back.

Perhaps there is a weak relationship between economic progress and political stability. If an economy stagnates and if unemployment is high, it is probably easier for opposition to be kindled, simply because idle hands are more likely to be mischievous ones.

Myth: The primary objective of Third World nations is to modernize their economies as rapidly as they can.

Reality: On the contrary, most Third World leaders have other goals and objectives. These include achieving greater national recognition and prestige in the international community; acquiring modern and advanced military equipment; pursuing ideological preferences;

and agitating for international redistribution of income rather than domestic economic growth.

If one looks at behavior rather than rhetoric, development is among the goals and priorities of most of the nations of the Third World, but not at the top of the list.

There is a paradox in all this: If development is accorded primary emphasis among national objectives, success seems to depend on imposing limits on the scope and character of government intervention. Few Third World leaders are willing to let go of the reins of control and unleash the market forces that can help their economies grow.

Postaudit

The only part of this essay that carries a touch of nostalgic irrelevance is the initial reference to Alec Haig's nomination as Reagan's first (and short-lived) Secretary of State.

5

Democracy in the Third World:
A Missing Ingredient

Winston Churchill's aphorism about democracy ("the worst form of government except for all the others") also applies to the Third World, although this application was probably not the author's intention. In any event, the problem in the Third World is not whether democracy would be better or worse, but rather how to get it launched in a manner that provides a fair test of Churchill's proposition.

Social scientists have written tomes about the formidable obstacles confronting nascent, or prenascent, Third World democracies, and the recent histories of the Philippines, Pakistan, Korea, and Indonesia, to cite a few examples, provide ample evidence of these difficulties.

Nevertheless, improving the chances that Third World democracy can succeed faces one major obstacle that has been largely overlooked in the past: What can an *ex*-president or *ex*-chief of state in a Third World country look forward to doing after he moves out of the presidential palace? In the absence of an answer that is both feasible and attractive, it is not surprising that Third World leaders as different as Marcos in the Philippines, Zia in Pakistan, Suharto in Indonesia, and Chun Doo Wan in Korea were willing, if not eager, to convince themselves, or be convinced by others, that the best interests of their countries required extending their tenure—whether by imposing martial law, amending or suspending the constitution, or rigging an impending election. Frequently, the result is that democracy is aborted, or continues to function as a discredited sham.

By way of comparison, consider the extraordinary range of opportunities open to ex-chiefs of state or ex-heads of government in

A slightly abbreviated version of this essay was published under the title "How to Put Autocrats Out to Pasture" in the Los Angeles Times *on February 9, 1986.*

the United States and other democracies in the developed world. For example, exiting leaders can write best-selling books and serve as newspaper and TV commentators (Nixon); they can join numerous corporate boards with lucrative retainers, and can be featured speakers at national and international meetings and conventions (Ford and Helmut Schmidt); they can establish university-based research and conference centers named after themselves (Carter).   And their presidential successors, as well as the media, typically seek their counsel on a more or less regular basis.

Besides the substantial income realized from such activities, ex-presidents may receive annual lifetime stipends ($69,000 plus $96,000 for office help, in the United States) as a result of their prior government service.   And all of this leaves ample time for golf, skiing, tennis, and softball!

Of course, this package still adds up to less than the challenge and excitement of the presidency. But the point is that there definitely is life after the White House, or after 10 Downing Street, or after the Elysee Palace. Indeed, the range of activities and income accessible to ex-presidents adds up to an appealing combination of financial security, personal stimulus, and public stature.

Now, consider the contrasting prospects facing the likes of Marcos, Zia, Chun, Suharto, and their genre, if they exit their present posts. The options are limited and unattractive. Corporate boards don't stand in a queue to invite their participation. Publishers don't compete for rights to their memoirs by offering lucrative advances and royalties. And the media don't clamor for their weekly or monthly comments. Moreover, their prior associates in government or the military typically avoid, rather than seek, their company, lest contact be viewed by the new incumbent as a sign of disloyalty or, worse, of a potential coup.

Thus, if a Third World ex-president continues to reside in his own country, he is likely to be ignored. If not ignored, he may be viewed as a thorn in the side of a successor whose tolerance for having him around may be limited. (Even lesser presidential challengers, like Benigno Aquino in the Philippines and Kim Dae Jung in South Korea, became personae non gratae to the reigning leadership.)

Exile, whether voluntary or induced, may then appear as preferable to the circumscribed, if not risky, prospects at home. (It is not surprising that Marcos may have acquired property in the United States and elsewhere, and that other Third World leaders have salted wealth abroad as insurance in case exile becomes their most attractive option.)

In sum, the options that are readily available to Third World ex-presidents are few and unattractive. Moreover, such options as do exist are likely to appear especially dismal by comparison with being head of state. The result is that incumbent leaders may contrive or conspire to prolong their tenure, resulting in the deferral and discrediting, if not demise, of one incipient democracy after another.

Can anything be done to remedy this situation? Not easily, for a clear and compelling reason: the absence of inviting prospects for postpresidential careers in Third World countries is rooted in their limited economic, technological, and social development. It is no less true that the abundant opportunities open to ex-leaders of democracies in the West and in Japan are rooted in their advanced economic, technological, and social development.

Yet this doesn't mean that successful democracy is bound to be a rare occurrence in Third World countries until their economies and societies attain a level of development more like that of the first world. At the least, a few concrete steps can ease the problem sooner.

For example, large private corporations and foundations (such as Ford, Rockefeller, MacArthur, Johnson) might consider Third World ex-presidents as possible directors or board members when their records in office and other credentials so warrant. And, within Third World countries themselves, certain institutional developments might improve the situation. For instance, in Korea, discussion and planning are fairly well advanced to establish a privately endowed "think tank" with an agenda for research and international conferencing relating to foreign policy and defense issues that might provide one or more prestigious positions to attract an outgoing Korean head of state. The process might also be helped by establishing reasonable stipends to support ex-presidents who exit their offices in accord with proper constitutional procedures.

Recognition of what has been a neglected problem can perhaps suggest some useful remedies. The result can be at least a modest improvement in prospects for the success of democracy in the Third World.

Postaudit

The gist of this message continues to be relevant, although some of the examples are obsolete. Indeed, the violence accompanying the removal of Marcos in 1986 and the assassination of Zia in 1988, in sharp contrast to the relative quiescence accompanying Chun Doo Wan's departure from Korea's presidency in 1988, reinforce the central point of the essay. The incentives affecting Chun's departure were essentially those alluded to in the essay, although his prior misdeeds and the antagonism of opponents with long memories prevented Chun from realizing the comfortable postpresidential life he aspired to.

6

Cooperative Forces in Third World Conflicts

In considering whether and how to respond to conflict contingencies in the Third World, the United States may have something to learn from the markedly different style of Soviet operations in such conflicts. Soviet operations have been characterized by a surprising degree of multilateralism, while those of the United States have often been characterized by a no less surprising degree of unilateralism.

This asymmetry arises because the Soviets have developed an effective network of cooperating "fraternal" communist states (such as Cuba, Vietnam, East Germany, Nicaragua, and North Korea), as well as supportive noncommunist states and entities having interests that partly converge with those of the Soviet Union (Libya, the PLO, Syria). These participants perform military as well as nonmilitary roles, and provide contributions in varying forms and amounts. Although the operational details are obscure, the players in this "Red Orchestra"[1] are usually conducted by the Soviet Union (more specifically by the International Department of the Soviet Communist Party), which also pays most of the bills.

The U.S. approach to conflict situations in the unstable Third World is quite different. Generally, when these situations arise, we properly give first consideration to whether or not the United States should be involved at all. If we thereafter consider whether or not to try to engage other partners in a cooperative effort, the focus is typically on

---

A slightly abbreviated version of this essay was published under the title "U.S. Could Use Its Own Cubans and East Germans" in the Wall Street Journal *on May 1, 1986.*

[1] The term "Red Orchestra" (rote Kapelle) was widely used to refer to the communist underground in Germany in World War II.

enlisting our European allies, usually with distinctly modest results. Our attempt to counter Libyan terrorism through cooperative pressure is only the latest example of this experience.

It is timely to examine the benefits and costs of a different approach: one that would encourage the development by friendly Third World countries of cooperating military and security forces capable of conducting, in cooperation with the United States and among themselves, low-intensity military operations and related support activities in the Third World, when the need arises. The purpose of this cooperative effort would be to contain and reverse communist imperialism in the Third World, to advance legitimate, indigenous, noncommunist liberation movements, and to further the mutual interests of the United States and its cooperators in promoting more pluralistic political systems in the Third World.

This approach has numerous precedents in prior U.S. activities. For example, employment of Korean combat units in Vietnam in the late 1960s; forming, equipping, and supporting the Meo hill tribes in Laos in the early 1960s; supporting freedom fighters in Afghanistan since 1980 (with Pakistan's cooperation); and the contras in Nicaragua since 1981.

"Cooperative forces" would be drawn from countries and movements within the Third World willing to act in concert with the United States for the advancement of mutual interests. Even granted that this mutuality would be only partial, it could permit some burdens to be shared between cooperating countries and the United States. The policy would be overt and explicit, although in some instances there might be reasons for implementing it through more quiet channels.

"Cooperative forces" are not "proxies" or "surrogates." Proxies act at the behest of a controlling power, which generally bears all of the accompanying costs. Cooperative forces would act from mutual interest, and therefore would be expected to share costs, responsibilities, and decisionmaking. Among possible cooperators are Egypt, Jordan, Morocco, Pakistan, Turkey, Venezuela, Brazil, Argentina, Korea, Indonesia, the Philippines, and Taiwan.

From the standpoint of potential Third World cooperators, several incentives might motivate participation: helping to deter, contain, or reverse a common threat; enhancing their regional and international influence and stature; and improving their military and related security capabilities.

From the U.S. standpoint, development of cooperative forces would also entail potential benefits: providing a means for sharing political as well as economic costs, and a way of reducing the gap between global U.S. interests and capabilities; and allowing for division of labor and some degree of specialization of functions between the United States and its associates. Such a partnership would also provide opportunities for complementarity in planning, equipping, and operating U.S. and cooperating forces in low-intensity conflicts.

In both deterring and conducting low-intensity conflict, cooperating countries might participate in various ways: providing training and equipment; offering maintenance and other forms of logistic support; extending limited financial support; and in some instances, providing small combat or security units. Differences in the forms and extent of participation may be accepted by different cooperators, as well as appropriate in such diverse situations as those exemplified by Angola, Nicaragua, Afghanistan, and Cambodia. A different type of multilateral, cooperative force might be appropriate to help a beleaguered, friendly Third World country like El Salvador. Annulling Libyan-supported terrorism might also be accomplished more effectively through employment of Third World cooperative forces.

Incremental costs of cooperative forces should be low for two reasons. First, cooperators would be expected to bear part of the costs because the endeavor is intended to be joint and the burden to be shared. Second, participation would become a major criterion in allocating the present level of Security Assistance funds, as well as the governing criterion for any additional funding authorized and appropriated for this purpose. Because Security Assistance funding would be a vehicle for jointly planning the forces and contributions of cooperating countries, as well as those of the United States, these funds could have a multiplier effect.

The Soviet Union has repeatedly asserted that its support for wars of national liberation in the Third World is quite compatible with improved U.S.-Soviet relations. The United States could adopt a similar stance. U.S support for cooperative forces need not preclude improvements in bilateral U.S.-Soviet relations and continued negotiations for mutual arms reductions.

A fair evaluation of the cooperative forces idea, and its subsequent translation into effective policy, cannot be accomplished easily or quickly. Meeting congressional and public concerns would require a persuasive argument that political as well as economic burdens will be shared, and that cooperative forces will reduce rather than increase the likelihood that U.S. combat forces will subsequently be engaged. Eliciting participation from prospective cooperating countries will depend on their assessment of the mutual benefits to be derived from this type of loosely structured security partnership. The likely concerns of our allies in Europe and Japan also warrant careful consideration.

Plainly, this would require further study and a serious multiyear effort if an effective network of cooperating elements were to be developed to meet the challenge of low-intensity conflicts in the Third World. In the process, the asymmetrical advantage hitherto realized by the Soviet Union through its "Red Orchestra" may be redressed by development of a "Blue" one.

Postaudit

Juxtaposing the case for cooperative forces to the Soviet Union's "Red Orchestra" is clearly asynchronous with the new thinking of perestroika *and U.S.-Soviet relations. However, the central theme of the piece remains relevant to the international environment of the 1990s. If and when occasions arise—as they are likely to—when the United States wishes to project power in the Third World, they are more likely than in the past to warrant cooperative actions in association with local and regional powers. U.S. policy formulation, as well as the configuration of military forces, will face an increasing need to operate in a cooperative and multinational, rather than unilateral, mode in the 1990s.*

7

International Debt and Arms Limitation

Not every cloud has a silver lining, but when one appears, it's worth attention. In this case, the cloud is the nearly one trillion dollars of international debt owed by the developing countries and Eastern Europe. The silver lining is the improved outlook for arms limitation that the cloud portends.

The arms likely to be limited aren't the nuclear weapons of the United States and the Soviet Union. They are instead the possibly more destabilizing and hardly less worrisome aircraft, missiles, artillery, armor, naval and surface weapons—about $30 billion of which are sold each year on the international weapons market, principally by the United States, the Soviet Union, and France, as well as other suppliers. More than three quarters of this amount is sold to developing countries.

In the past, this market has been fueled by two sources of finance: credit, extended by the governments and commercial banks of supplier countries; and dollar earnings of oil exporting countries, used either to buy weapons directly or to finance purchases by others. The two sources have often been linked because some of the earnings of the oil exporters were loaned or given by them to other arms buyers (as with Saudi Arabia's subventions to Syria), or were intermediated by OPEC's depository banks in the West in the form of loans to supposedly credit-worthy borrowers, often resulting directly or indirectly in financing arms purchases.

A slightly abbreviated version of this essay was published under the title "Nations' Heavy Debts May Mean Less Traffic in Arms" by the Los Angeles Times *on March 19, 1984.*

Currently, the precarious predicament of international debtors and creditors foreshadows a significant reduction in the availability of cash and credit for weapon purchases. And the erosion of OPEC earnings, due to continued slack in oil prices and sales, will further restrain financing available for weapon purchases.

Between 1971 and 1980, military equipment valued at about $200 billion (expressed in constant 1979 prices) was traded on world markets, of which 75 percent was imported by developing countries. In 1980, one third of total sales was imported by countries of the Middle East, 19 percent by Africa, 13 percent by Asia, and 10 percent by Latin America. About 50 percent of the total was financed by credit. Arms sales were usually sweetened by substantial subsidies provided through below-market interest rates, long grace periods and amortization schedules, government insurance of commercial bank credits, supplier price rebates, and various combinations of these inducements.

The situation currently facing sellers and buyers has changed dramatically. Prospective buyers will, in general, have more limited access to international credit for two reasons: because petrodollars will not be flowing into international financial markets in such profusion as they did a few years earlier, and because international bankers and foreign governments are now more aware that repayment prospects are in many cases much bleaker than was believed to be the case in the 1970s and early 1980s. Prospective sellers now must realize that future arms sales will have to be more heavily subsidized than in the past because of the reduced liquidity and precarious solvency of prospective buyers. Larger subsidies and reduced prospects of repayment essentially imply diminished economic incentives to sell.

Of course, both political and economic considerations will limit the force of this argument. For example, some prospective buyers, like Saudi Arabia, will still have ample means to finance arms imports (as reflected by the Saudis' recent agreement to pay $4 billion over several years for an advanced air defense system to be provided by France). And the major supplying countries, notably the United States and the Soviet Union, will have sufficiently strong political reasons to continue supplying arms to such countries as Israel, Egypt, and El Salvador, in the U.S. case, and Cuba and Syria, in the Soviet case, notwithstanding deterioration in the prospects of repayment by these recipients. For the Soviets, this general deterioration in repayment prospects will be particularly burdensome because its arms sales in recent years have been a lucrative source of cherished hard currency earnings—to a much greater extent than has been true for the United States.

Nevertheless, while the arms traffic certainly will continue, the prognosis is for its level to decrease significantly in the coming years. This may not always be beneficial. In some cases weapons modernization and improvement can increase military stability: the military balance on the Korean peninsula is a case in point. However, on the whole, diminished arms traffic is generally to be preferred to its increase, and the debt overhead is likely to place a damper on the weapons market.

There is a silver lining to the international financial cloud, even if it's not spectacular.

Postaudit

In the late 1980s, the silver lining I had envisioned in 1984 was still thin and dim. Global arms sales in 1987 were $47 billion, only slightly below the level of the early 1980s (in 1987 prices). Over 80 percent of the 1987 total was imported by developing countries. Evidently, the principal arms sellers have not yet allowed the cloud of international debt to interfere significantly with continued sales. Instead, suppliers have eased the terms and increased the subsidies they provide to enable "sales" to continue!

8

"Star Wars" and the Economies of Western Europe

It is no secret that prevailing European attitudes toward the Strategic Defense Initiative ("Star Wars") are acutely ambivalent.

On the one hand—the political and military one—the Europeans are somewhere between skeptical and hostile to both the concept of strategic defense and to its likely consequences. On the other hand—the economic and commercial one—the Europeans are, by and large, seriously concerned about the danger of being left behind technologically if they don't participate in SDI, or in the putatively parallel but demilitarized R&D program proposed by the French—"Eureka."

European opposition to SDI is based on two somewhat inconsistent themes. If SDI works technically, and is "cost-effective" operationally (which means that the increased costs of improving strategic defenses turn out to be less than the increased costs of offensive forces needed to counter such improvements), the Europeans fear the United States and the Soviets might work out a deal between them that would leave Western Europe more exposed to the risk of conventional war. If SDI does *not* work—an outcome the Europeans believe is much more likely—they fear the result would be a ratcheting upward of the arms race, heightened East-West tensions, and insufficient attention to improvements in NATO's conventional military capabilities.

Associated with these reservations is an argument viewed by many Europeans as the clincher: SDI is not only undesirable for the reasons noted, it is also unnecessary; 40 years of nuclear peace have resulted

A slightly abbreviated version of this essay was published under the title "SDI Is No European Elixir" in the Wall Street Journal *on October 23, 1985.*

from the deterrent effect of mutual assured destruction *without* effective defenses—post hoc, ergo propter hoc is the contention—so why rock the boat?

Notwithstanding their profound reservations, and quite apart from the merits of these arguments, the Europeans are nevertheless tempted by SDI for an entirely nonmilitary reason: They think it may provide the cutting edge of new technology and a much-needed stimulus to the disappointing rates of growth in output and employment of their ailing economies. A recent commentary by John Newhouse conveys this somewhat starry-eyed view:

> Some Europeans are saying that . . . Star Wars won't budge very far from Square One militarily . . . but the commercial spinoff from all that money spent on the most awesome technologies could be immense: phrases like "third industrial revolution" are bandied about. . . . Star Wars will have an even greater impact on high technology commerce in the years ahead than the Apollo program had in the nineteen-sixties and seventies.

The sober truth is that such hopes are distinctly unwarranted and unrealistic. The ills that beset the Western European economies won't be allayed, let alone cured, by participation either in SDI or in Europe's own planned space research effort, the Eureka program. Actually, Eureka suffers from a further lapse of logic. Eureka is based on two implicit premises: first, Star Wars technology is likely to generate major commercial spinoffs; and second, these spinoffs will be more accessible to American firms that participate in SDI than European firms that do not. (Note that this second premise implies that the potential commercial spinoffs from SDI would be appropriable by participants, but *not available to "free riders."*) The conclusion is then erroneously drawn that Western Europe should have a parallel but demilitarized program, to develop similar technologies and thereby avoid being placed at a technological disadvantage relative to American firms participating in SDI.

Eureka's lapse of logic is simply this: If there were likely to be substantial commercial payoffs from these technologies, *and* if they were appropriable, then there would be no reason for government financing of the R&D in the first place! Private firms would have powerful incentives to do the job on their own. Only if the principal payoffs from the technology were military, rather than commercial, would government financing be justified in the first place.

In any event, there are several reasons why these "awesome technologies"—whether from Star Wars or from Eureka—won't much help the European economies. One reason is that the programs themselves will be highly capital-intensive and brain-intensive. Employment and output effects will be exceedingly limited, and largely confined to a very small segment of engineering and science professionals in research laboratories, experimental "skunk-works," and testing ranges. Subsequent impacts on employment and growth are very uncertain, probably quite small if they occur at all (in fact, the results are more likely to be labor-saving than labor-using), and surely postponed until the very remote future.

The other reasons relate principally to the fact that Western Europe's main economic problems derive from structural and institutional conditions quite independent of Star Wars technologies and most unlikely to be affected by them.

In the past decade, annual rates of GNP growth in the Western European economies have fallen from an average of more than 3 percent in the 1976 to 1980 period to less than 1 percent in the 1980 to 1985 period. In the last half of the 1980s, these rates have risen slightly. During the same time, European unemployment rates have risen from an average of less than 6 percent to more than 9 percent. (Unemployment rates in the United Kingdom and the Benelux countries are about 10 or 11 percent, and in France, West Germany, and Italy, in the 7 to 9 percent range.)

Although many factors contribute to this disappointing performance, the two principal causes are fairly clear. First, diminished economic growth has been heavily influenced by a very substantial increase in the size of the public sector in Western Europe relative to the market sector. Second, the sharp rise in unemployment has been heavily influenced by a substantial increase in European wages relative to productivity.

Public sector expenditures have risen from less than 40 percent of Western Europe's aggregate GNP at the start of the 1970s to 50 percent currently. Empirical analyses done at the World Bank for the decade of the 1970s and at The RAND Corporation for the 1972 to

1982 period show a statistically significant *negative* relationship between economic growth and expansion of the nonmarket (government) sector relative to the market sector. According to this statistical relationship, the substantial rise that has occurred in the share of European GNP represented by public sector expenditures—itself attributable to fundamental political and social conditions prevailing in Western Europe—explains about half the reduction in Europe's rate of economic growth occurring in the past decade.

The sharp rise in Western Europe's unemployment rate has, in turn, been principally due to increases in real, or inflation-adjusted, wages that have exceeded increases in labor productivity. This disparity has occurred because nominal wages have been fully indexed to cost-of-living changes, and because politically sensitive governments and party coalitions have allowed or encouraged additional wage and nonwage benefits irrespective of productivity growth. As a result, real wages in Western Europe have risen in the past decade by one third relative to wages in the United States, where more flexible labor market conditions have prevailed. And employment in Western Europe has remained nearly constant since 1975, while increasing by more than 18 million in the United States during the same time period.

If these underlying causes of Western Europe's economic difficulties are remedied, the sclerotic performance of the European economies will be improved. If they're not remedied, Europe's economic outlook will remain clouded. In any event, the remedies and their prospects are quite independent of SDI or Eureka. Neither program should be sold as a means of easing Europe's fundamental economic problems. Such hoped-for effects will not occur, and if the programs' supporters encourage or indulge these unrealistic hopes, disappointment and recriminations will ensue in the future, and will then further weaken the NATO alliance. Those who support the alliance should not encourage European participation in either SDI or Eureka by holding out a prospect of economic and commercial benefits from these programs that are most unlikely to ensue.

If European (and for that matter, Japanese) participation is to occur at all, the best way to bring it about is for governments to avoid placing unnecessary obstacles in its path. Allowing for special handling where classified research may be involved, European firms, laboratories, scientists, and engineers wishing to participate in the R&D program—*given* the defense-related purpose that motivates it—should be allowed to compete and cooperate as they are able and willing, without either endorsement or opposition by their governments.   The NATO governments would, of course, have the opportunity and the obligation to decide upon their participation in SDI if and as deployable, cost-effective defensive systems emerge.

Postaudit

The main points of this piece remain valid: namely, the commercial spinoffs from SDI research have been distinctly limited, and the European Eureka program hasn't had any appreciable effect in reducing unemployment in the European economies. However, the discussion plainly erred in failing to see the prospective emergence of the European Community in 1992, and of course the dramatic changes that have occurred in Eastern Europe and in the scaling down of the Soviet threat.

The Soviet Union and China

9

Talk in Moscow, Action in Beijing

Actions do not always speak louder than words. While the media has devoted meticulous attention to each twist and turn in Soviet pronouncements on "restructuring," there has been relative neglect of the truly significant actions and experiments undertaken by the Chinese to bring about genuine reform.

As a result of this contrast, perestroika has become a multilingual synonym for systemic restructuring, while its Chinese counterpart, Gai Ge, is virtually unknown outside China.

The Soviets have spoken louder and more often about reform; the Chinese are, simply and pragmatically, doing it. To be sure, it remains uncertain whether and to what extent the Chinese will succeed; if they do, how long success will last; and if it does last, what its effects on the Communist system will be. But at least their efforts are tangible and visible, actions rather than words.

When the Soviet Union was holding its nineteenth party conference at the end of June and the beginning of July 1988, with 5,000 delegates and 250 speakers providing high theater in Moscow, I was in Beijing doing consulting work on one aspect of China's reform. At the time, both the Western and Chinese media were filled with details about the Moscow conference: Gorbachev's proposals to place more executive power in the hands of government while reducing that of the party; to shift party activity from micromanaging the economy to establishing policy (as though policy and execution can be readily separated); to consider whether, as part of this realignment, responsibility for defense and foreign policy should be lodged with the government's chief executive, rather than the Politburo; and to determine whether the chief executive should be titled "president" or

A slightly abbreviated version of this essay was published under the title "Perestroika Gets Headlines, but Gai Ge Has the Get-Up-and-Go" in the Los Angeles Times _on October 5, 1988._

"chairman." (On the premise that Mr. Gorbachev intends to fill this position as well as that of the party general secretary, the ironic result of this "reform" will be to concentrate more power in one man's hands than at any time since Stalin!)

Although the party conference provided one more indication of the remarkable change in the Soviet atmosphere—the importance of glasnost shouldn't be minimized—the plain fact is that not much in the way of genuine system transformation has occurred in the Soviet Union. While words have been plentiful, actions have been quite limited.

In contrast to the rhetoric in Moscow, what has been under way in Beijing is much more significant and fundamental, as well as much less reported and understood outside China. For example, the Chinese in April established Hainan Island as China's fifth and most "special" Special Economic Zone (SEZ). Along with the other four SEZs, the new province of Hainan is explicitly intended to be an experiment in creating an economic environment that would borrow from the development experience of Hong Kong, South Korea, and Taiwan. The Hainan innovations include a loosening of the Beijing bureaucracy's tight control over the provincial Hainan government, providing 70-year land lease arrangements and special tax advantages to encourage foreign investment.

In the SEZs, as well as in such trade-oriented coastal provinces as Guangdong, several thousand joint ventures, partly financed with foreign capital, are already in operation, compared with less than a few dozen in the Soviet Union. In China, fundamental market-oriented policies are actively discussed at the highest levels: for example, to relate prices to economic costs; to gear wages and salaries to productivity rather than seniority; and to acknowledge that savings, accumulation, profits, and property rights are essential elements in system reform. The issues that arise in China relate less to the desirability of moving in these directions, than to their timing, sequence, and the extent of the remaining nonmarket sector.

Of course, Gai Ge has been under way since the end of the 1970s, and perestroika only since 1985. Nevertheless, over a roughly comparable span, genuine reform moved much farther in China than it has in the Soviet Union. By 1984, China had abolished the communes, launched the "responsibility system" in Sichuan that produced a surge of small-holder agricultural production, and reportedly increased individual commercial enterprises tenfold. Most of the corresponding stirrings in the Soviet Union have been in the realm of pronouncements, proposals, and decrees rather than tangible actions.

To be sure, it remains uncertain how either Deng Xiaoping's or Gorbachev's reform efforts will work out in the long run. Opposition exists in both China and the Soviet Union, but even this provides an instructive contrast. In China, the recently reported opposition to Gai Ge relates to the short-term price effects of market-oriented *actions*. In the Soviet Union, critics are of two quite different types: those who criticize the *absence* of action, and those who fear the consequences if it occurs.

In any event, there's little doubt which reform effort has the better chance of moving forward. Perestroika in the Soviet Union is still a pallid counterpart to Gai Ge in China. Moscow may be where the publicity is. Beijing is where the action is.

Postaudit

The significant error of this piece is its obvious lack of clairvoyance about the bloody events near Tiananmen Square in Beijing on June 3 and 4, 1989, and the political repression that followed it. Notwithstanding this tragedy and the economic retrenchment that followed, there remains in 1990 more reality and substance in China's economic reform than in that of the Soviet Union.

10

Consensus and Dissensus about the Soviets

Coauthored with Henry S. Rowen

Seldom has there been such uniformity of expert opinion as there currently is concerning the conditions and prospects of the Soviet Union. Yet ironically, this consensus has not diminished, and perhaps has even intensified, prevailing disagreements about preferred U.S. and Western policies.

The present consensus concerning Soviet conditions is based on a reasonably solid body of facts and accepted inferences:

- *Economic growth.* Between 1971 and 1986, Soviet economic growth has persistently declined, and the growth of aggregate productivity has decreased or been negative. According to the Soviet Union's own estimates, annual growth of national product declined from 5.7 percent in 1971 to 1975 to 4.2 percent in 1976 to 1980, and to 3.4 percent in 1981 to 1985. The corresponding U.S. government estimates are 3.8, 2.7, and 2.2 percent. Independent estimates by the authors and several other analysts suggest even lower growth rates. Soviet growth targets for the 1986 to 1990 period are about 4 percent per annum, while the prevailing consensus among Western analysts is that the actual figure is more likely to be about 2 percent and probably even lower, signifying near stagnation in per-capita terms.

An abbreviated version of this essay was published under the title "On Soviets We Agree to Disagree" in the Los Angeles Times *on January 20, 1987.*

- *Hard currency earnings.* Soviet hard currency earnings have declined in the past two years by about 30 percent, from $32 billion in 1984 to $22 billion in 1986, mainly due to lower oil prices and to some reduction of Soviet hard currency arms sales. As a result, Soviet borrowing from the West has risen sharply, and is likely to continue at a high level.

- *Military spending and military power.* Growth of Soviet military spending has apparently slackened somewhat, just about keeping pace with the reduced growth of Soviet national output. Official U.S. estimates of the burden imposed by Soviet military spending suggest a share between 15 and 17 percent of Soviet GNP, and there are reasons for believing that the actual burden is even higher. Our own estimates are in the neighborhood of 25 percent. Notwithstanding the slower growth of military spending, Soviet military power is formidable as a result of both accumulated military expenditures in prior years as well as the high levels of current outlays.

- *Social conditions.* Alone among the world's industrial countries, the Soviet Union has experienced an increase in infant mortality and an unprecedented decline in life expectancy between the end of the 1960s and the early 1980s. Moreover, the decline was due not only to the aging of the Soviet population, but to a rise in age-specific death rates across age groups. As Mikhail Bernstam has pointed out, among the large number of Soviet ethnic groups, the Russian population has been the most severely affected by this deterioration. During the same period, there has also been a sharp increase in alcoholism in the population as a whole.

- *Politics.* Despite the bear's evident sickness, the control exercised by the Soviet ruling class—the *nomenklatura*—remains firmly anchored in the party and its supporting pillars of power: the KGB and the military.

The aforementioned consensus among putative Soviet experts is less clear on the question of whether, and in what ways, Gorbachev wants to reform the Soviet economic system. Nevertheless, there is general agreement that his ability to change the system—quite apart from his wishes—is severely limited by the fundamental clash between the requirements for maintaining centralized political control and the requirements for increasing incentives, decontrolling information access, and decentralizing opportunities, that would be at the core of genuine reform.

If there is general agreement about these prevailing conditions, what are the policy differences, and why do they persist?

At the risk of some oversimplification, the policy differences can be divided between two broad orientations: "detente-minus" and "containment-plus."

The detente-minus position harkens to the 1970s era of detente, which it views with some nostalgia, occasionally mixed with an acknowledgment, as well as mild criticism, that the benefits of detente in the past were perhaps too one-sided. According to this position, a new and updated version of detente could realize a better balance through harder bargaining on the part of the West, and tighter "linkage" between Western "quids" and Soviet "quos." The West would thus benefit more, and give up less, than in the 1970s detente: hence, "detente-minus." Among those holding this position are West German Foreign Minister Hans Dietrich Genscher, many of our European allies, former Secretary of State Cyrus Vance, and many members of Congress and of the State Department.

Detente-minus acknowledges that the Soviet Union is a hostile adversary, with values inimical to those of the West. However, according to this policy stance, we can "do business" with the Soviet Union because it shares with us a mutual interest in avoiding war, is genuinely anxious to avoid confrontation, and is less inclined than in the 1970s to expand its empire in what is, in any event, the relatively less important Third World arena. The detente-minus position views the Soviet Union as more or less similar to other nations in seeking to advance its national interests, and therefore willing to make and to adhere to agreements that reflect these interests.

Based on these assumptions, the policies favored by adherents of detente-minus include arms control agreements (with SDI favored as a bargaining chip to be traded for lower offensive force levels), increased economic relations with the Soviet Union encouraged by subsidies where necessary, expanded "dialogue" on a wide range of economic, scientific, and technological matters, and general acceptance of the Marxist-Leninist states that have arisen in the Third World as well as ones that may arise in the future.

The containment-plus stance harkens back to the earlier 1950s and 1960s theme of the younger George Kennan (his views have changed rather sharply since the 1947 Mr. X article). Whereas the original formulation of containment envisaged military, political, and economic resistance to expansion of the Soviet empire, the newer version would add prudent efforts both to *reverse* the expansion in the overseas empire that occurred in the 1970s, and to alter the most noxious and secretive aspects of the Soviet system itself; hence containment-plus. This position was held by President Reagan, his key cabinet and subcabinet aides, some members of the Congress, and Zbigniew Brzezinski.

Containment-plus views the Soviet Union as an "evil empire" (the adjective is currently not fashionable, although the concept remains influential), which may alter its tactics but not its basic and irreconcilable long-term aim: namely, to "bury" capitalist democracy. According to this policy stance, the Soviet Union, because of the priority it accords to military power and the empire, as well as its obsession with secrecy, centralized political control, and the coercive power of the secret police, cannot abide a nonconflictual, open, international environment. Containment-plus tends to view the only common interests between the Soviet Union and the West as confined to the avoidance of a major war and the control of nuclear proliferation.

The containment-plus view opposes the use of SDI as a standard bargaining chip to further arms control negotiations, and instead urges accelerated and sustained research and development of strategic defense capabilities. Other policies favored by containment-plus include implementation of the Reagan doctrine through support for "freedom fighters" and cooperative forces to reverse the Soviet empire in the Third World, as well as expanded information programs to reach and influence the peoples of the Soviet Union and of its extended empire. Adherents of containment-plus would limit economic relations with the Soviets, confining them to ones that are strictly unsubsidized.

Of course, there are shadings within, and combinations between, detente-minus and containment-plus. There is even occasional movement between them: for example, Henry Kissinger, the original architect of detente in the 1970s, currently occupies containment-plus ground.

The fundamental disagreement between detente-minus and containment-plus rests on their basically different assumptions concerning the *proper* objectives of U.S. and Western policy and the *actual* objectives and character of the Soviet Union. That the deep policy disagreements associated with these two positions remain unaffected by agreement concerning Soviet economic, social, political, and military conditions follows unsurprisingly from the depth of the disagreements and their underlying assumptions. The persistence of such sharp disagreements among putative foreign policy experts suggests what psychologists refer to as "cognitive dissonance": if convictions are held strongly enough, they can abide a very wide range of unexpected and seemingly contradictory events without undergoing change.

In foreign policy, expertise may thus contribute more to agreement on diagnosis than agreement on prescription. The latter requires the exercise of judgment, and that of the public may be as good as or better than that of the experts.

Postaudit

From the vantage point of 1990, some of the issues of 1987, when this piece was written, appear less relevant if not irrelevant, while others appear clearer in retrospect than they did at the time. The pessimists about Soviet economic performance were clearly closer to the truth than the optimists, although even the pessimists may have been too optimistic. The "evil empire" is in shambles. Glasnost and the political side of perestroika have acquired a visibility and momentum that are as unexpected as the relative absence of the economic side of perestroika. And the policy disagreements have narrowed, although not disappeared. Everyone is now more or less detentiste. The remaining disagreements relate to whether and to what extent U.S. policy should support Gorbachev personally, or instead should support him only when the actions he takes resonate with American values, opposing him when they don't. In general, the detente-minus folk of 1987 have tended to be "Gorbachev's-our-man" supporters in 1990, while the containment-plus people have become supporters of actions first and Gorbachev second, if at all!

11

The Underlying Disagreement about
How to Deal with the Soviet Union

With growing prospects that the United States and the Soviet Union will start talking in a few months about antisatellite weapons, it's timely to consider why experts on the Soviet Union with apparently equal qualifications so often disagree sharply on how to deal with the Soviets.

Consider the expertise represented by the following pairs of individuals and institutions: George Kennan and Paul Nitze; Cyrus Vance and Zbigniew Brzezinski; Marshall Shulman and Richard Pipes; Tom Wicker and William Safire; the *New York Times* and the *Wall Street Journal*; the Foreign Service and the military services; the Brookings Institution and the Hoover Institution. Policies favored by each member of these pairs typically and predictably differ from those favored by the other member. Moreover, the differences apply equally to issues drawn from the past (should the SALT II agreement have been ratified?), the present (should some concessions be offered by the United States to persuade the Soviets to resume the START negotiations?), and the future (should arms control agreements with the Soviets be sought in the absence of strict verification provisions, or should credits to the Soviets be encouraged by Western governments to expand East-West trade and to improve East-West relations?).

These persistent differences are accounted for by fundamentally differing beliefs or premises about the nature of the Soviet system and the principal objectives of its leadership. The contrasting beliefs can be usefully characterized as "mirror-imaging" (MI) and "power-maximizing" (PM), representing opposite ends of a spectrum along which are arrayed the members of the previously cited pairs. (In each

A slightly abbreviated version of this essay was published under the title "Why the Experts Disagree About the Soviets" by the Washington Post *on July 25, 1984.*

49

pair, the first member is situated at or close to the mirror-imaging end of the spectrum, while the second member is at or close to the power-maximizing end.)

Of course, the MI-PM dichotomy is an oversimplification. Positions are often more complex than this strict binary choice implies; various nuances and combinations do occur. Nevertheless, the distinction conveys something that is crucial for explaining and anticipating the sharply different stances taken by experts as well as by nonexperts, including presidential candidates.

The mirror-imaging view of the Soviet system and its leadership holds that apparent Soviet aggressiveness, expansionism, and preoccupation with enhanced military capabilities, are reflections of Russian history and culture. These preoccupations, it is acknowledged, may border on paranoia and consequently may take aggressive forms. However, such manifestations are considered by mirror-imagers to be understandable reactions to Soviet and Russian history, including the experience of Western efforts to abort the Bolshevik Revolution, the 20 million casualties suffered by the Soviet Union in World War II, and the periodic devastation experienced by Russia at the hands of foreign invaders. Preoccupation with military strength, and the priority given to resource allocations for the military, are to be explained, according to the mirror-imaging view, mainly by this historical legacy.

Nevertheless, according to MI, the long-term aims of the Soviet Union have something in common with our own: human betterment and well being, social progress, peace, prosperity, and social justice. Hence, according to adherents of MI, a more forthcoming Western policy—one that combines concessions with firmness—is likely to produce over time a symmetrical rather than an exploitative response from the Soviet leadership, and perhaps also an irenic evolution of the Soviet system. In the absence of such concessions, mirror-imagers tend to view prospective Soviet behavior with concern if not alarm, lest a hostile international environment, combined with increased Soviet economic stringency at home, arouse the Soviets' latent paranoia and provoke Soviet aggression. These presumed Soviet behavioral responses to alternative Western policies are the core of the mirror-imaging view.

By contrast, the power-maximizing view holds that, whatever the grim experiences of Soviet and Russian history, and whatever the philosophical and ideological antecedents of Soviet communism, the overriding objective of the system is to maximize the political and military power of the Soviet state at home and to expand it abroad. According to power-maximizers, Gorbachev's "new thinking" represents a sharp change in means and in style rather than in fundamental goals. Hence, concessions made to the Soviets and agreements and transactions with them, are fair game for exploitation and deception in the interests of maximizing Soviet power and expansion. The PM position denies, or at least seriously doubts, that economic and social betterment are important goals of the system as it really operates. Instead, holders of this position view the deferral of these goals as readily acceptable to the Soviet leadership, perhaps even obscurely welcomed by it, because of the overriding preference for strengthening Soviet vigilance and power in response to the alleged ubiquity of external and internal threats.

Differences between the mirror-imaging and power-maximizing views lead to predictable differences in the policies that their adherents advocate. For example, mirror-imagers tend to look with favor on negotiations that are initiated or facilitated by Western concessions, and trade that is expanded by using, if necessary, one or another type of subsidy. By contrast, power-maximizers tend to favor negotiations without any initial concessions, and trade without any subsidies, preferring no negotiations to concessionary ones and no trade or limited trade to subsidized trade. Power-maximizers tend to emphasize the zero-sum nature of negotiations and other transactions with the Soviet Union (what the Soviets gain, the West and the United States lose), while mirror-imagers tend to emphasize the positive-sum character of such transactions (both sides can gain from them.)

Unfortunately, there is no way to provide a definitive test of which of these views—mirror-imaging or power-maximizing—is closer to the truth. Consequently, one is forced to rely on impressions, judgments, and experience—on insight as much as on eyesight—to make up one's mind.

One can also adopt a "hedging" strategy that tries to minimize regret. For example, suppose you pick the mirror-imaging view, then how badly off are we if that view is wrong? If instead you go with the power-maximizers, then how badly off are we if this view is wrong? So, one basis for choosing is simply to minimize how badly off we are if the view we adopt is wrong!

As the presidential campaign moves into high gear, differences between the candidates and their party platforms on this issue will be clear enough, even if the roundabout rhetoric that's employed sometimes tries to straddle both positions. In choosing between the two positions, a reflective person should proceed the same way that porcupines make love: carefully!

Postaudit

The debates and disagreements described in this piece have largely been overtaken by events. They are now of historical rather than current interest. Neither "mirror-imagers" nor "power-maximizers" anticipated the course of political reform in the Soviet Union since 1984, yet each is inclined to think that its view of the Soviets explains why the system was bound to change: the MI-group because the Soviets really wanted to and aspired to do so all along; the PM-group because U.S. and Western policy effectively prevented them from continuing what they had been doing.

There is a current issue about which disagreement among Soviet experts can be (inexactly) traced to the MI versus PM disagreement. This issue concerns whether U.S. policy should support Gorbachev personally (*because he provides the best chance of making the Soviet Union into a "normal" state), or should primarily support specific programs and actions, endorsing Gorbachev only when he endorses them and withholding support and instead expressing criticism when he does not.*

Generally, the former MI-group supports the man, *while the PM-group supports* programs.

12

The Coming Debate over Western Lending to the Soviet Union

If and as the current international debt predicament is brought under some degree of control, influential members of the business, financial, and media communities in the United States and Western Europe will convince themselves that Western lending to the Soviet Union should be encouraged. They will then try to convince others, as well as to influence government policies in the same direction. A debate will ensue whose manifest content will focus on economic considerations, although its underlying assumptions and motives will be fundamentally political.

The politics of the argument—the pros and cons of more extensive economic relations with the Soviet Union—will be a repetition of what has been frequently, if inconclusively, debated in the past. What will be new are the economic and financial contentions: specifically, the putative creditworthiness of the Soviet Union and its apparently favorable credentials among potential international borrowers. Just as it is current U.S. policy to allow, and even actively encourage *unsubsidized* East-West trade (excluding trade in military-related technology), as reflected in the recent U.S.-Soviet grain agreement, so, it will be argued, lending to the Soviets on normal commercial terms should be encouraged as well.

This scenario has acquired added verisimilitude in light of the special appeal in the West of Mr. Gorbachev's rhetoric and personality.[1] Consequently, it is pertinent to evaluate the economic arguments that will be made in favor of expanded lending to the

---

A slightly abbreviated version of this essay was published under the title "When Bankers Start Looking to Moscow" by the Wall Street Journal *on November 28, 1983.*

[1] This comment has been added to the original 1983 article.

Soviets, for these are the terms in which the foreseeable debate will be formulated.

On first glance, the argument is not without merit. Between the middle of 1981 and 1983, the Soviet Union's gross hard currency debt to Western commercial banks declined slightly from $14.1 to $13.9 billion, while its hard currency deposits in Western banks rose substantially, from $3.6 to $10.0 billion (probably due in considerable measure to increased Soviet gold sales). Thus, in the past two years, *net* Soviet commercial bank debt actually fell from $10.5 billion to only $4.0 billion. If government debt, which is largely in the form of short-term export credits, is added to these figures, Soviet gross debt is about $21 billion, and its net debt is $11 billion. [By the late 1980s, the corresponding figures had risen to $50 billion and about $40 billion, respectively.] Interest and principal payments on these debts currently absorb about 25 percent of Soviet hard-currency export earnings, a figure that is small when compared not only to the corresponding percentages for such precariously situated debtors as Poland, Brazil, Mexico, and Argentina, but also to such relatively reliable borrowers as France and Italy.

Viewed through the lenses bankers typically use in appraising financial risk, this would seem to establish the Soviet Union as a creditworthy borrower. This view will be especially congenial to the international departments of some of the world's major banks because its adoption might help to compensate for their sharply reduced lending activity in Latin America and Eastern Europe. By comparison with other potential international borrowers, it will be suggested, the Soviets deserve an A rating!

From this reasoning, the argument will be carried one step further. If the Soviets themselves appear reluctant to borrow (whether for reasons of financial conservatism on their part, or for more subtle negotiatory ones), Western bankers should, it will be argued, undertake to "market" loans to the Soviet Union: that is, persuade its leadership to borrow Western money. To help lubricate the process, various types of government subsidy will be advocated: for example, loan guarantees, export credit insurance, or tax preferment extended by Western governments to promote financial and trade transactions with the Soviet Union.

Now let's consider some possible flaws in the argument.

The Soviet Union's hard currency balance of international payments, and hence its creditworthiness, is unusually sensitive to the behavior of four commodities: three on the export side (energy—principally oil—arms, and gold); and one on the import side (grain). Prospects for all of these are extremely tenuous over the next several years.

Among the Soviets' three major hard currency exports, energy is by far the largest, comprising over 55 percent of its annual hard currency export revenues of about $30 billion.   World market prospects for oil are also the most precarious of the three. The 15 percent decline in nominal oil prices in 1983 compelled the Soviets to increase the volume of their oil exports to avoid the loss of hard currency revenues that would otherwise have ensued. Their ability to compensate for continued softness in world oil prices in the future by increasing the volume of exports of natural gas is likely to provide only a partial offset.

Hard currency arms sales in the mid- and late 1980s are also likely to drop. In the late 1970s and early 1980s, Soviet arms sales were typically $7 or $8 billion annually. OPEC surplus revenues, which in the past have directly or indirectly fueled the arms market, aren't likely to be available to do so in the 1980s, and the current world debt predicament will have a further damping effect on credits to finance arms sales. Hence, the outlook for Soviet hard currency earnings from this source too are unpromising.

Finally, while gold prices may fluctuate in the coming years, their prospects are not bright. Gold prices tend to move with inflation: When inflation advances, gold prices advance still faster; when inflation recedes, so do gold prices. Hence, the prospect that global inflation will continue to diminish compared with the past decade suggests that current annual Soviet earnings of $2.0 to $2.5 billion from gold sales are more likely to fall than to rise in the future.

Turning to grain imports, Soviet agreements with Canada and Argentina, as well as with the United States, obligate it to import a minimum of 18.5 million metric tons per annum over the next five years. The maximum imports allowed under the U.S.-Soviet agreement would raise this figure to 21.5 million tons. In addition, the Soviets have imported more than 3 million tons annually from Australia in recent years, and are more likely to increase than to reduce this in the future. Thus, annual Soviet grain imports from all suppliers are likely to be not less than 25 million tons, and may be as high as 35 or even 50 million tons, depending on the vagaries of weather and Soviet agricultural performance. Depending on world grain prices—also a profoundly uncertain factor—Soviet requirements for hard currency to finance its essential grain imports will be between $5 and $8 billion annually, and perhaps even more. When further allowance is made for the hard-currency costs of "normal" Soviet imports of machinery, non-grain food, and raw materials, as well as the continued, albeit constrained, costs of the Soviet Union's external empire, the financial picture that emerges is cloudy indeed.

In sum, the Soviet Union is a much more risky borrower than would seem indicated by the types of data bankers typically look at. Especially in light of the past decade's demonstration that the judgments of international bankers are remarkably fallible, the debate on Western lending to the Soviet Union should be treated with abundant caution and limited credulity. Based on the economics of the case, to say nothing of the politics, "cash on the barrelhead" is a more prudent policy for the West to follow in transactions with the Soviet Union than lending money to it.

Postaudit

This piece was ahead of its time! The argument it makes is more current now than when it was written. Early in 1990, the Soviets attempted to float a 500 million Deutschemark Eurobond at a rate of 8 7/8 percent. The issue was soon discounted to 10 percent—implying a 13 percent adjustment for the increased riskiness of hard currency lending to the Soviet Union!

13

The Costs of the Soviet Empire

The costs of empire impose a burden on the Soviet economy. Along with numerous other more familiar factors, these costs have contributed to its sharply diminished performance. The costs translate into appreciable reductions in potential growth of Soviet civil consumption or military production. Yet such burdensome consequences have in the past been viewed by the Kremlin as imperative because of the broader political purposes the empire is believed to serve.

Many of the major questions associated with the Soviet empire cannot be answered conclusively, but considerable light is shed by recent RAND research on its costs during the 1971 to 1980 decade.[1] To start with, "empire" and "costs" must be defined. In a geographic sense, there are three Soviet empires: the empire within the boundaries of the Soviet state, the geographically contiguous empire, and the empire farther abroad. European writers usually have the first of these definitions in mind when they use the term: namely, the multinational Soviet state consisting of 15 distinct national republics and over 60 nationalities. The definition used here focuses instead on the *external* parts of the empire: the contiguous countries of Eastern Europe and Afghanistan; and the countries abroad which, unlike those of Eastern Europe, had not previously experienced Russian influence or control. This second part of the external empire includes Cuba, Vietnam, Angola, South Yemen, Ethiopia, Mozambique, Libya, Syria, Nicaragua, and North Korea.

A slightly abbreviated version of this essay was published by the Wall Street Journal *on January 30, 1984.*

[1] See Charles Wolf, Jr., K. C. Yeh, Edmund Brunner, et al., *The Costs of the Soviet Empire,* Santa Monica, The RAND Corporation, R-3073/1-NA, September 1983.

Clearly, this definition covers a wide variety of situations: satellites, allies, spheres of Soviet influence, and more or less friendly, if not fraternal, states. Yet this variety is entirely consistent with the characteristics of the Roman, Ottoman, British, French, Japanese, and other empires of the past. Hobson's classic study of the 19th-century British empire referred to "quibbles" over the definition of "empire" and the "sliding scale of political terminology" applied to it. The term is used here in the same sense to cover all the various forms of political sway and influence exercised by the Soviet Union, at a cost to its economy.

Moreover, some costs that are properly attributable to the empire may be incurred in and on countries that are not currently within it. For example, costs may be incurred in countries that are targets for expanding the empire's domain in the future (such as India), or for thwarting and disrupting opposition to its future expansion; Soviet support for covert destabilization activities in Turkey is an example of this latter type of cost.

In sum, empire costs have encompassed those costs incurred by the Soviet Union to maintain or increase its control in countries it already dominates, to acquire influence perhaps leading to future control in countries that seem promising candidates, and to thwart or subvert countries opposed to it.

The principal components of these costs are: (1) implicit trade subsidies covering both the underpricing relative to world market prices of Soviet exports, such as oil, to Eastern Europe, Cuba, and Vietnam, and the premiums above world market prices paid by the Soviets for imports, such as Cuban sugar, from these countries; (2) export credits extended by the Soviet Union with doubtful prospects of repayment; (3) Soviet military aid deliveries, net of hard currency military sales; (4) economic aid deliveries net of repayments; (5) incremental costs of Soviet military operations in Afghanistan until the withdrawal of Soviet forces in February 1989, and the continuing costs of supporting the Najibullah government since that time; and (6) costs of Soviet covert, destabilization activities in the third world.

With the single exception of military operations in Afghanistan, the following estimates exclude the costs of Soviet military forces, even though large elements of these forces (for example, the 32 Soviet divisions in Eastern Europe and the tremendous expansion in recent years of Soviet naval forces) clearly contribute to the Soviet imperial enterprise. The reason for this exclusion is that these military forces also contribute to defense of the Soviet state; hence, imputation to the empire of some part of their total cost would inevitably be arbitrary.

Clearly, enormous data problems bedevil these estimates. But the bottom line, even if blurred, is interesting and substantial. In constant 1981 dollars, using official exchange rates, costs of the Soviet empire rose from about $18 billion in 1971 to $24 billion in 1976 and about $41 billion in 1980, an annual growth rate of nearly 9 percent for the decade as a whole. As a proportion of published CIA estimates of Soviet GNP, the costs of empire rose from about 1.1 percent in 1971 to approximately 2.7 percent at the end of the decade, averaging 1.6 percent over the period. As a ratio to Soviet military spending, the costs of empire rose from 9 to 19 percent during the decade, averaging about 13 percent.

The picture is even more striking if these data are expressed in rubles rather than dollars. The ruble figures are relatively much larger than the dollar figures when the hard currency parts of empire costs are converted to rubles at realistic, rather than official, exchange rates. (Realistic rates represent the ratios between internal ruble prices and external dollar prices of Soviet hard currency imports during each year of the past decade.) Expressed thus in rubles, with which the Soviets carry on the bulk of their economic activity, the costs of empire rose from 1.8 percent of Soviet ruble GNP in 1971 to 3.6 percent in 1976 and 6.6 percent in 1980, averaging 3.5 percent for the decade as a whole. As a ratio to Soviet military spending, costs in rubles rose from 14 percent in 1971 to 28 percent in 1976, and 50 percent in 1980, averaging 28 percent. The annual average growth rate of the ruble costs of empire was over 16 percent for the decade.

Are the Soviet costs of empire large or small? Obviously, the answer depends on the criteria one adopts.

Costs are clearly twice as large in rubles as in dollars, relative to Soviet GNP. And it is the larger measurement that probably reflects the calculus of Soviet decisionmakers.

The Soviet empire burden is also very large compared with the roughly corresponding categories of U.S. costs, covering U.S. economic aid, military aid, and official export credits. As a share of the respective GNPs, the Soviet cost in dollars was over three times the comparable U.S. figure, and in rubles was over eight times the U.S. figure during the past decade.

Another sizing criterion is the burden imposed on the Soviet economy—evidently another of the numerous factors contributing to the declining performance of the Soviet economy in recent years. As a crude measure of this burden, each increase of 1 percent in the annual share of empire costs in Soviet GNP translates into a reduction of between 0.6 and 1 percent in the annual growth rate of Soviet military production, or about 0.3 percent in annual growth in civil consumption. For example, if empire costs rose from an annual level of, say, 1 to 6 percent of Soviet GNP, annual consumption growth would be reduced by about 1.5 percent. Alternatively, such an increase would reduce annual growth in military production by about 3 or 4 percent. [2]

The ultimate criterion is, of course, not economic, but political and strategic. How large do the costs of empire appear relative to the political and strategic benefits attributed to the empire by the Soviet leadership? Plainly, this most significant criterion for evaluating Soviet empire costs is also the least measurable. It encompasses both tangible elements, such as bases in Cuba, Vietnam, and elsewhere, that increase the effectiveness of Soviet military forces, as well as less tangible but perhaps even more important elements, such as international political prestige, Russian national pride, the ideological imperative of "assisting" the inevitable march of history toward communist domination, and a putative justification in the leadership's eyes for the sacrifices imposed by the Soviet system on its populace. (That this justification is unlikely to be persuasive to Soviet consumers is both true and immaterial.) In the aggregate, these benefits of empire may, from the Politburo's viewpoint, amply justify its costs. They suggest that Soviet efforts to expand the empire are likely to continue.

The Soviet Union's imperial phase has been aptly described by Milovan Djilas on the basis of his long experience with communism in the Soviet Union and Yugoslavia:

> Soviet communism . . . is a military empire. It was transformed into a
> military empire in Stalin's time. Internally, such structures usually

---

[2] Since Mr. Gorbachev's assumption of power in 1985, the costs of supporting the empire have been more tightly controlled as a result of both increased awareness of the severity of the Soviet economic predicament and of the "new thinking" and rhetoric in Soviet foreign policy. Even at reduced levels, empire costs still absorb perhaps 2 to 3 percent of the Soviet GNP.

rot; . . . but to avoid internal problems, they may go for expansion. . .
If it is stopped, the process of rotting will go faster.

Postaudit

That the cost of empire was large, as well as a significant contributor to the changes represented by perestroika, is now generally accepted. It was not part of the conventional wisdom when the piece was written.

14

Prospects for the Soviet Empire

What are the prospects for demise of the Soviet Empire, or for its survival and expansion?

Six or eight years ago the question would have seemed irrelevant, and its answer obvious. Survival of the Soviet system at home and its continued control in Eastern Europe were taken for granted. At the same time, expansion of its influence and control abroad seemed unthreatening, as well as slow and uneven. Now the question is distinctly relevant and timely, and its answer neither obvious nor certain.

One plausible answer is, from the U.S. point of view, guardedly optimistic. Not since the early years following the Russian revolution of 1917 have the fundamental weaknesses and vulnerabilities of the Soviet system been as evident as they currently are. Soviet economic growth has sharply declined from an annual average of about 5 percent in the 1960s to less than 2 percent in the 1970s. For the 1980s, the prospects are for a further decline. Labor productivity has also declined, while increasing inputs of capital have been accompanied by diminished yields in both industry and agriculture.

In social terms, the system has fared still worse. Among developed countries, the Soviet Union is unique in showing *increased* mortality rates for its population as a whole over the past decade, as well as a *decline* in life expectancy. Infant mortality has risen by 50 percent in the past decade, and is currently three times that of the United States.

While its economic and social performance have thus deteriorated, the brutishness with which the system crushed political dissent remained unchanged (until the advent of perestroika and glasnost after

A slightly abbreviated version of this essay was published under the title "Soviet Empire-Builders Push On—How Far Will They Go?" by the Los Angeles Times *on February 24, 1982.*

1985). In the process, the Soviet system lost whatever economic, social, or political appeal it might once have offered for foreign emulation. As a consequence, clear and increasing signs have appeared of divisiveness within its established domain in Eastern Europe, and in other parts of its empire outside Europe. Poland is, of course, the most dramatic example in the political realm. Romania's deviant foreign policy, and Hungary's economic experimentation with market incentives as well as its emerging experimentation with political pluralism, provide other examples of divergence and restiveness.

Furthermore, the costs of sustaining the Soviet Union's expanded imperial domain have grown enormously to an amount that may be one fifth as large as its total military expenditures. These costs include subsidies on export and import trade with Eastern Europe and other client states, economic and military aid, and military operating costs in support of Cuban and East German proxy forces. They don't include the potentially large additional costs that may impinge on the Soviet Union as a residual guarantor of the $70 billion of Polish and other East European external debt.

In light of the system's economic and social shortcomings at home, and the restiveness and rising costs associated with its expansion abroad, the cohesion and sustainability of the Soviet empire would now seem uncertain.

Unfortunately, this is only one plausible answer to the original question. A quite different, more pessimistic answer is also plausible.

While its social and economic performance has deteriorated sharply in the past decade, the Soviet Union has achieved dramatic success in expanding its military power: in strategic forces, tactical forces, and external projection forces; in naval, ground, and air forces; in conventional as well as nuclear forces. With its massive growth of military power as a backup, the Soviet Union has developed an effective formula for expanding its empire, a formula that seems not much affected by the flaws of the parent system or the empire's rising costs.

This formula begins with the inevitable and intractable tensions and instabilities—social, economic, ethnic, and political—in the Third World, and even in parts of the "first" world. In these troubled waters, the Soviet Union has successfully navigated, by employing a wide range of policy instruments to expand its domain: trade subsidies and direct economic and financial assistance; grants and credits for weapons; training and logistic support for Cuban and East German proxy forces for combat; internal security and police roles in Africa and the Middle East; and, in exceptional circumstances such as Afghanistan, Soviet occupation forces as well.

The formula has been applied in a selective, pragmatic, and controlled manner to expand Soviet influence in Angola, Ethiopia, South Yemen, Vietnam, Cambodia, Laos, Benin, Madagascar, Congo-Brazzaville, Nicaragua, Syria, and Libya, while maintaining Soviet dominion in Eastern Europe, Cuba, and North Korea. While there have been some Soviet setbacks (Somalia and Egypt, and the growth of splintering tendencies in Poland and Hungary) during this period, the gains realized by the Soviet empire have vastly exceeded its losses. Neither the disarray in the Western alliance, nor the U.S. defense build-up in the early and mid-1980s, provides a reason to think this process will be reversed.

Which of the two plausible answers is more realistic?

Certainly, the Kremlin leadership under Gorbachev is more keenly aware than ever before of the formidable costs, fractiousness, and burdens of empire. And certainly the myriad difficulties and short-falls within the Soviet system seem likely to increase and to warrant more resources and attention at home.

Yet there is every reason to think that maintenance of the empire still rates high among the values cherished by Soviet leaders. And there is no reason to think they have permanently decided to eschew efforts and costs to propitiate the empire's further growth. Moreover, the process of further expansion through support for "fraternal" states can be so contrived and manipulated by the leadership that failure to pursue it is itself viewed as a threat to the Soviet Union, while persisting in doing so both preempts the threat and extenuates the need for economic and social sacrifices at home. Rather than viewing Afghanistan or Poland as halting the course of expansion, subsequent Soviet leaders may view them as difficulties that have been managed satisfactorily, albeit painfully.

With disunity rife in the Western alliance, and U.S. foreign and defense policies yet to provide an effective counterweight, it is erroneous to think that the Soviet empire has reached its peak, and even more in error to think its position is precarious—like that facing the Romans when Alaric and the Goths laid siege to the city.

Realism probably lies between the pessimistic and the optimistic answers.

Postaudit

The first half of this essay was surely prescient. The second half surely less so, although the story hasn't yet fully played out. At the least, the pessimistic half of the piece perhaps explains the empire's maintenance through most of the 1980s.

15

Soviet Economy and U.S. "Opportunity"

Coauthored with Henry S. Rowen

The idea that the sick Soviet economy compels Moscow to seek a new arms pact with the United States is in fashion. Sovietologist Seweryn Bialer says in *Forbes*, "Never in the past 20 years did they want arms control as badly as today." Peter Tarnoff of the Council on Foreign Relations says in the *New York Times*, "We can exact better arms-control terms from Moscow today than at any previous time in the two Reagan Administrations." Others see a "historic opportunity." Our own views, which emphasize the long-run drag on Soviet military power from continued poor economic performance, have been (wrongly) interpreted in a similar vein by some people.

Reality here is complex. The Soviets do face troubles that could, in the most hopeful analysis, lead to a cut in arms and force a turn to serious economic liberalization at some point. But in the meantime, a Moscow regime could sustain its military effort and even veer toward re-Stalinization out of desperation. And, though a slowdown in the Russian military build-up might be a part of any transition steps, the West must remember that strategic superiority in arms is a crucial element in the design of the Soviet system. This ought to wave caution flags in front of those here who look to arms agreements and expansion of trade as a bridge to peace.

Mikhail Gorbachev is quoted (in samizdat) as calling his economy "a mess." And despite his efforts, it's likely to keep doing poorly. Contributing to the slowdown has been the large and rising share of resources devoted to the military and to extending the Soviet empire via the use of proxy states.

This essay was published in the Wall Street Journal *on December 11, 1986.*

Faced with this severe pinch, Moscow is pushing an arms-control strategy—so successful in the past in restraining the United States—to buy it time to regroup domestically while yielding no part of its global military position. The emphasis is on stopping the Strategic Defense Initiative, but its aims are much broader. Important Soviet policymakers see a need to increase the nation's capacity for high-tech warfare, largely conventional but also nuclear. This can be a particularly expensive task, one ill-suited to present harsh economic realities. The deus ex machina could be a transfer of critical Western technology and capital, and inducements for the United States to hold back its own military modernization.

For several decades, Soviet economic growth has been slowing; over the past decade, U.S. government estimates show it at a little over 2 percent annually. We and some other analysts think it might have been lower. Planned growth for 1986 to 1990 is about 4 percent, while many Western analysts believe it really will be about 2 percent and perhaps lower, signifying near stagnation in per-capita terms.

One third or more of additional national output went to the Soviet military or empire over the past decade. By now, they absorb more than 20 percent of the Soviet gross national product (versus less than 8 percent for the United States). The payoffs have been a much-strengthened military position, the ability to conduct a war in Afghanistan without noticeably weakening strength elsewhere, and support for the Cubans, Sandinistas, Vietnamese, and other members of the empire. Evidently, the Politburo judged the gains to have been worth the high costs. There is little reason to believe that Mr. Gorbachev and the other new men value these power benefits less than did their predecessors.

But they face a serious problem: If they can't get the country's economy moving ahead, sooner or later something will have to give. (It might be Mr. Gorbachev's tenure in office.) The present effort to improve productivity, largely through discipline and new bosses, is unlikely to work for more than a short time at best. What follows then? Even more Stalinist discipline would meet strong internal opposition. Market decentralization, Chinese style, would help, but such a move would be strongly resisted by the nomenklatura, much of which is digging in its heels at Mr. Gorbachev's largely modest changes. (The recent legalizing of private service activities is a significant step, but prohibiting the hiring of any labor shows the strength of the resistance to change.) Less military spending would help realize Mr. Gorbachev's capital plant-modernization goals, but people who take pride in overtaking the West militarily want to build on, not abandon, that achievement.

Hence the appeal of a revived detente that would help bring in more technology and capital, undermine support for military spending in the West, and lessen the need for heavier Soviet military spending while increasing the payoffs from any new military programs undertaken.

This strategy worked in the 1970s. The Soviets made a great leap forward in military power and in extending the empire not only through their own vigorous efforts but also because their enemies relaxed. The United States took the accords on ballistic missiles and missile defenses as a general signal to spend less on arms and to develop fewer weapons systems. For example, the number of known Soviet systems deployed in the first half of the 1980s—which reflected new projects put in development during the detente of the 1970s—was twice that of the United States.

The story of the 1980s is different. By the end of the 1970s, the Soviet detente or arms-control strategy was eroding and almost met its demise with the invasion of Afghanistan. Since then, the United States has recovered somewhat militarily, the overseas parts of the Soviet empire are under challenge on all fronts, and the Soviet economy is in deep trouble.

To the Soviets, the 1970s are a better model, and we are seeing an attempt to revive it. The Soviet leadership has reason, once again, to be hopeful. Congress, which slowed research on more accurate guidance for missiles for a period in the 1970s, now prohibits testing of antisatellite weapons, strictly limits production of chemical weapons, favors a narrowly restrictive interpretation of testing of antimissile defenses under the ABM treaty, and has threatened to impose a one-year moratorium on all nuclear tests. Self-limitation, which borders on paralysis in some areas, has not been confined to Congress. It was the executive branch that chose not to deploy the neutron bomb in Europe after the Europeans had agreed to it and long-neglected improvements in the command-and-control systems.

Internally, the Soviet leadership faces a more complex choice than guns versus butter. It is nuclear missiles (and defenses against Western ones) versus conventional weapons (especially higher-technology ones and those capable of delivering both nuclear and conventional munitions) versus supporting embattled members of the empire versus investment goods versus consumption goods. In the internal struggles, a coalition may exist between some in the military and the economic modernizers on the merit of investing more in high-tech, flexible capital equipment even at the expense of reduced weapons procurement now in order to be able to produce better weapons later.

A precedent is Khrushchev's move in the 1950s to reduce the army, create the strategic rocket force, and cut military spending (then increase it in the 1960s). Now there are similar pulls in these and other directions, and no one knows how they will be resolved in the short run. But unless economic performance improves over the long run, a decade or more, the Soviet Union will lose ground militarily.

One pull that has been widely noted in the West is toward giving higher priority to nonnuclear forces. Former Chief of Staff Marshall Ogarkov is interpreted as advocating this—with a strong nuclear backup. But the savings realizable from this shift are likely to be small, because the Soviets spend much less on nuclear than conventional forces. And if they slow the pace of modernizing their nuclear forces and have a smaller number, they might still end up spending more on these forces because of the new weapons' higher cost.

They clearly don't want to face the array of advanced technologies that the SDI could produce. Better to get the United States to abandon these defensive efforts (as it did in the 1970s) or persuade Washington to wrap them in a web of constraints. On form, these constraints would be rigorously monitored and enforced by the American press and political system.

We may indeed have a "historic opportunity." But given the record of earlier agreements and what we know about the Soviet internal situation, this "opportunity" may be no more than a way of facilitating a Soviet switch in military strategy and the bolstering of this adversary's capacity for a more diversified arms challenge. Instead of relaxing and relieving Moscow, the West should do its best to leave the Kremlin with only one viable option: dealing with its internal problems by spending less on the military and the empire and taking further and bolder privatizing steps.

Postaudit

The principal time-warp that mars this piece is its complete failure to mention the extraordinary developments in Central and Eastern Europe in 1989, and the connection between them and the unfolding economic predicament in the Soviet Union.

The policy prescription offered in conclusion seems, in retrospect, to have been both close to what was pursued, as well as generally effective.

16

"Guns Versus Butter" in Gorbachev's Reforms

Coauthored with Henry S. Rowen

Current conventional wisdom about the Soviet Union embraces two propositions. First, the Soviet economy has suffered serious and protracted economic setbacks; second, as a consequence, the leadership wants to reduce the country's heavy military burden to help reverse the trend and facilitate the progress of perestroika.

In fact, the available evidence warrants much greater confidence in the first proposition—the Soviet economy's serious predicament— than the second "guns-versus-butter" part.

Indications of the economic predicament are numerous and mutually reinforcing. Soviet economic growth, though relatively high in the early 1970s, has been declining steadily since then. While estimates differ, all of them place recent growth at very low rates (around 1 to 3 percent per annum). The lower estimates are probably more accurate, and also are probably better indicators of what lies ahead. They imply either stagnation or decline in per-capita Soviet GNP.

Furthermore, Soviet hard currency earnings have been sharply reduced since the early 1980s by the decline in prices of the Soviet Union's two principal exports, oil and weapons. As a result, hard currency earnings have declined by more than one third since 1984. To offset these losses, Soviet international borrowing has risen to at least $5 or $6 billion per year, and its total international debt has increased by two thirds to over $40 billion since 1985.

A slightly abbreviated version of this essay was published under the title "Gorbachev's Choice Isn't Just Guns or Butter" in the Wall Street Journal *on March 24, 1988.*

Gorbachev's own statements convey a message even starker than that suggested by these numbers:

> In the latter half of the 1970s . . . the country began to lose momentum. Economic failures became more frequent. . . . Elements of stagnation began to appear in the life of society. . . . The gap in the efficiency of production, quality of products, scientific and technological development began to widen. . . . A sizable portion of the national wealth became idle capital. . . . There are glaring shortcomings in our health services . . . and there were difficulties in the supply of foodstuffs, housing, consumer goods and services.

In contrast to the substantial evidence on the economic predicament, evidence in support of the "guns versus butter" idea is distinctly limited. Gorbachev's book, *Perestroika: New Thinking for Our Country and the World*, contains a few hints. For example, he observes that "in discussions with Americans and people from other Western countries, I always ask bluntly if they want the Soviet Union to have a chance to direct more of its resources to economical and social development through cuts in its military spending."

But these hints are ambiguous and insubstantial, even though the idea may acquire substance in the future.

However, it's worth bearing in mind that other, more complex, as well as less frequently discussed, options may be chosen by the Soviet leadership, rather than the simple choice between guns and butter.

For example, to the extent that Soviet interest in arms control—INF or strategic—is motivated by economic considerations, these may be due not to a desire to transfer resources from military to civil uses, but rather from nuclear to conventional forces: from intermediate or strategic nuclear systems to improved battlefield command, control, and communications; or to airlift; or surveillance.

Even potential reductions in Soviet conventional forces might be welcomed by the Soviets not for the purpose of freeing resources for nonmilitary uses, but rather to provide resources for more modern, more mobile, and more effective, albeit smaller, forces.

Another plausible option within the military domain is something that might be called "guns today versus better ones tomorrow": that is, reallocating resources from present forces to permit an increase in research, development, testing, and production capacity to obtain higher-tech systems in the future, such as standoff weapons, "stealthy" platforms, and precision-guided munitions—in the process helping to close the gap between U.S. and Soviet technology in these fields.

And still a third option for the Soviets is to save military resources within the Soviet Union while diverting them to other parts of the empire. The large boost in Soviet arms shipments to Cuba, Nicaragua, and Angola in the past year, and the possibility of something similar in Zimbabwe, are cases in point. Soviet withdrawal from Afghanistan could be a notable counterexample unless it is accompanied or followed by substantial military deliveries to the successor regime.

These examples share a common characteristic: reallocations from some military-related uses to others, rather than to increase nonmilitary consumption or nonmilitary investment. Thus, they represent not guns for butter but guns of one type, time, or place for those of another.

Guns versus butter may be in Gorbachev's eventual plans, but there are several reasons for doubting it. One reason is the military's role as an integral part of the machinery of Soviet state power since its inception, a role that has been certified in Soviet revolutionary history as well as in Lenin's writings and doctrine. It is worth remembering that Gorbachev never tires of reminding us that he is a staunch Leninist.

Moreover, Soviet economic planning has characteristically accorded special priority to military needs, reflecting guidelines that were laid down in early Soviet history by Marshall Mikhail Frunze, one of the strongest and most influential Soviet military chiefs in the 1920s. With Lenin's blessing, Frunze established the rule that the military's needs should, without question, receive top economic priority in Soviet economic planning. Besides the immediate and direct needs of the military, it was intended that precedence should be given to those other branches of industry that produced outputs of joint use in the military as well as nonmilitary sectors, and to nonmilitary industry that could be rapidly converted to military uses. These rules and traditions have become firmly grounded in Soviet thinking, planning, and behavior over the last six decades. They are unlikely to change rapidly, if at all.

In addition, recent Soviet military writings display a keen recognition of the impending revolution in military technology, as noted in the recent report by the U.S. Commission on Integrated Long-Term Strategy. New technology is likely to change the fundamental character of warfare in the next two decades. The greater precision, range, and destructiveness of weapons could extend war across a much wider geographic area; make war much more rapid and intense; and place a premium on surveillance, intelligence, detection, and concealment. It seems unlikely that the party leadership, including Mr. Gorbachev, does not endorse the aspirations and efforts of Marshal Akhromeev and other top military commanders to move vigorously to develop and acquire these new technologies.

Finally, recent empirical research at RAND suggests that a strong, large, and technologically well-developed military sector seems to be a statistically significant attribute of communist systems, compared to noncommunist ones. It is possible but doubtful that this general characteristic, and in particular the singular accomplishment it has represented in the Soviet Union, would be sacrificed by the Soviet leadership or curtailed by perestroika.

Of course, it may turn out that the Soviet Union's "new thinking" will lead to a guns-for-butter tradeoff. But it would be chancy and dangerous for U.S. and Western policymakers and publics to bank on it. It would be safer and wiser to assume that what Gorbachev has in mind is something else: namely, that perestroika and its associated economic reforms can contribute to improving the functioning of the Soviet economy as a whole, while the Soviet military's priority access to aggregate resources and to advanced technologies will be unchanged, if not actually increased.

Postaudit

Although the last word on this has certainly not been written, the piece doesn't stand up well to the test of time. Gorbachev has made some cuts in military resource allocations, and additional ones probably impend. Moreover, political developments in Central and Eastern Europe, the pending drawdown of Soviet forces in Eastern Europe, the progress of arms control negotiations (especially the likely asymmetrical cutback of Soviet conventional forces in Europe) and the development of Soviet military doctrine in the direction of "defensive defense"—all of these changes since 1988 suggest that the conclusion was overly pessimistic.

17

What Cuts in Soviet Military Spending Can Do for Perestroika

Mikhail Gorbachev's recently announced plan for unilateral reductions in Soviet military spending and military forces raises a question as to the plan's prospective gains and losses. The answer depends on whether assessment of gains and losses is made in political, economic, or military terms.

Soviet political gains will probably be large in the international arena, and uncertain internally in the Soviet Union. Surprisingly, economic gains will probably be small. And any military losses that ensue will probably be small, short run, and subject to reversal.

Gorbachev has proposed unilateral reductions of 10 percent in active forces including 10,000 tanks, half of which would be in Eastern Europe; 14 percent in military spending (from an unspecified base); and 19 percent in military procurement.

Prospective Soviet political gains in the international arena are likely to be both evident and substantial, as a result of these cuts. These gains probably include the imposition of added strains on both parts of the U.S. alliance system—NATO and Japan—because the West Europeans are inclined to attribute much greater significance to the planned cuts than is the United States, while the Japanese are inclined to attribute much less significance to them. Gorbachev's external political gains also include delay, if not deferral, of conventional force modernization in NATO, increased congressional and public pressure to reduce the U.S. defense budget, and a further roiling of the already troubled discussions that the United States is having over "burden sharing" with both NATO and Japan. Soviet military cuts will also tend to encourage the West Europeans to

---

A slightly abbreviated version of this essay was published under the title "Soviet Military Cuts: Who Wins? Who Loses?" in the Wall Street Journal *on February 21, 1989.*

expand capital flows and trade with the Soviet Union, providing a further source of friction within the alliance.

Political effects within the Soviet Union would be less clear: disappointment if not opposition within some parts of the military and the party, and encouragement and support among perestroika's backers in the party, among intellectuals, and in the public.

Economically, the Gorbachev plan appears to be a clear and welcome indication of a "guns versus butter" tradeoff: the transfer of resources from the military to provide consumer benefits, worker incentives, and increased labor productivity, thereby building political support for General Secretary/President Gorbachev's reforms. With an aggregate military and national security effort costing as much as 25 percent of the Soviet gross national product, the scope for such tradeoffs would seem to be very large. Yet this raises a crucial issue for perestroika: the extent to which the Soviet Union's acute economic predicament—which Gorbachev himself has characterized as "precrisis" in character—is due to the enormous Soviet military burden or instead to fundamental systemic flaws and contradictions, that a transfer of resources from the military would leave unchanged. Of course, both influences are involved in the Soviet predicament. At issue is their relative importance.

In fact, when one looks at the numbers and makes realistic assumptions about the potential Soviet military cutbacks, it is surprising how small the immediate and short-term direct effects of the proposed cuts would be.

For example, if one assumes as an upper-bound a cut of 20 percent in aggregate Soviet defense resource allocations over a three- to four-year period, the total transfer of resources from the military to the civil sector would represent 5 percent of the Soviet GNP. Because consumption in the Soviet Union is approximately 60 percent of its GNP, this transfer of "guns" would amount to an aggregate 8.5 percent increase in "butter" for the benefit of the Soviet consumer. In very gross terms, per-capita consumption in the Soviet Union is probably in the neighborhood of about $3,600 to $4,000 (compared with about $14,000 in the United States), so the transfer would amount to between $300 and $340 per capita over a three- or four-year period.

Allowing for perhaps a 1 percent annual rate of population increase would further reduce the per-capita increase in consumption to about $200 over the period when the military cuts are being implemented.

Moreover, this cumulative increase would represent a one-time shift, not a continuing increase at this rate. And if instead of devoting the savings from reduced "guns" entirely to consumption, some of the resource transfers were devoted to investment in consumer goods production, or to research and development, the realized rate of increase in "butter" would be still further reduced over the three- or four-year period, although the prospect for further increases thereafter would be enhanced.

While these calculations are extremely rough, they lead to the conclusion that the direct economic benefits from the guns-versus-butter tradeoff that Gorbachev has proposed are likely to be quite modest.

Correspondingly, the reductions in military capabilities that a cut of this scale would entail are also likely to be modest. For example, the savings in military resources could be realized by reducing second echelon Soviet ground forces, redundant strategic rocket forces, and naval forces, while leaving the air forces, air defense forces, and Soviet space efforts intact. Other options are also available for limiting the effects of cuts on major military capabilities. Moreover, some of the savings might be used not to trade off guns for butter, but to trade off lower-technology guns today for higher-technology weapons in the future.

For Gorbachev, the result of the proposed cuts would probably mean both good news and bad news. The good news is that the political gains from the proposed measures would probably be large while the military losses would be small. The disappointing news is that the economic gains would be small, while the need for fundamental systemic changes in incentives, market prices, enterprises, property rights, public finance, and currency convertibility would remain unchanged and no less essential if any substantial improvement in growth, productivity, and consumer well-being is to be achieved.

For the West, there's also good news and bad news. The bad news lies in the serious political stresses and strains noted earlier, which can contribute to erosion of the western alliances. The good news is that Gorbachev's guns-versus-butter tradeoffs, without effective system reform, could somewhat reduce the Soviet military threat in the short run, while opening up prospects of further threat reductions in the future, and leaving unaffected the underlying economic and technological weakness of the Soviet system. In an uncertain world, the guns-versus-butter tradeoff without system reform may be preferable to the systemic reform without the guns-versus-butter tradeoff.

Postaudit

The probable effects of reduced military spending without systemic reform remain largely as described in this essay. Some of the estimates used in the calculations have been improved, and are presented in the next essay (on Gorbachev's "peace dividend"), but the general conclusion remains unchanged.

18

Gorbachev's Peace Dividend

The potential Soviet "peace dividend" is very large relative to that of the United States, yet its effect in raising living standards for the average Soviet consumer will probably be surprisingly small.

Explaining this apparent paradox depends on several estimates and assumptions: first, the current level of Soviet military spending, and a plausible estimate of its potential reduction; second, the current share of aggregate consumption in the Soviet GNP, and an estimate of the current level of Soviet per capita consumption; and third, the annual rate of population growth in the Soviet Union.

Spending for the military and for security-related purposes as a percentage of Soviet GNP has been variously estimated as 9 percent (by Soviet Premier Ryzhkov), 16 percent (by the CIA), and about 25 percent (by a small group of independent scholars, sometimes referred to outside and inside government as "Team B").

With respect to potential cuts, Gorbachev announced last year a plan for reductions of 14.2 percent in military spending over a period of several years.

This background provides a basis for bounding the potential Soviet peace dividend. It is reasonable to assume a current level of Soviet military spending of at least 20 percent of the Soviet GNP (about four times that of the United States), a cut in this figure of perhaps 25 percent over a four-year period (nearly twice what Gorbachev has proposed), and a transfer of the resulting "dividend" of 5 percent of the GNP to boost living standards for the sorely tried Soviet consumer.

Aggregate consumption in the Soviet Union is between 50 and 55 percent of GNP, so these potential resource transfers from military to

A slightly abbreviated version of this essay was published by the Wall Street Journal *under the title "Meager Peace Dividend for Soviets" on April 12, 1990.*

civilian consumption uses would represent an increase of about 10 percent over the four-year period, or 2.25 percent per year. Inasmuch as the Soviet Union's 285 million population is growing at an annual rate of about 1 percent, the ensuing boost in per-capita consumption would be 1.25 percent annually, cumulating to a 5 percent total increase by 1995.

In dollar terms, average Soviet per-capita consumption is about $3,000, approximately the same as that of Mexico and Turkey. Consequently, if the Soviet peace dividend were to be allocated in accordance with the prior assumptions, the average Soviet consumer would realize a distinctly modest annual increase in consumption of about $40, or about $160 over the specified four-year period. Moreover, this would be a one-time increase, settling at this plateau in 1995 in the absence of other changes in the Soviet economy. (If part of this potential dividend were devoted to investment in consumer goods industry rather than to raising consumption directly, the initial boost to consumption would be smaller than the previous estimate, but prospects for further growth after 1995 would be greater.)

To be sure, these illustrative calculations assume that the economic aspects of perestroika remain about as fixed on dead center as they have been for most of Gorbachev's tenure since 1985. Thus, no significant reforms are assumed to take place with respect to price deregulation, control of the money supply, imposition of fiscal discipline, privatization of state enterprises (perhaps to absorb a substantial part of the so-called ruble "overhang" of about 400 to 500 billion rubles), property rights reform, and currency convertibility.

If, on the other hand, these several key ingredients of systemic economic reform were vigorously implemented, prospects for significant betterment of the consumer's lot would be substantially improved—*even in the absence of as large a peace dividend from military cuts* as I have assumed.

Of course, Soviet options are not limited to one or the other of these choices. An effective combination between military cuts and economic reform would be more likely to produce substantial benefits for the Soviet consumer than either alone. But by itself, the peace dividend won't do very much.

These rough calculations have implications for planning by both governments and businesses in the West and Japan. To the extent that the experience and expectations of Soviet consumers (and voters) will affect political as well as economic prospects for stability and progress in the Soviet Union, the peace dividend alone won't contribute a lot. Systemic economic reform is required. Yet the Soviet record on this score has been unimpressive. In contrast to the significant political reforms instituted during the past five years, the economic dimensions of perestroika have featured rhetoric and illusion rather than action. In the absence of significant economic reform, assistance by foreign governments is likely to be wasted, while loans or investments by foreign businesses are likely to be risky and unrewarding.

19

Helping Mr. Gorbachev

Those who believe it is in U.S. and Western interests that economic reform in the Soviet Union succeed have misdirected their attention. They have proposed Western credits, direct investments, joint ventures, technology transfer, most-favored-nation benefits, and Soviet participation in international economic organizations. But prospects for the success of perestroika do not depend on these instruments. Success depends instead on rapid price reform: moving speedily from reliance on administered prices toward market-determined ones. With price reform, and regardless of Western help, Soviet resource allocations will improve, and output, productivity, and living standards will rise. Without it, external help will be ineffectual.

Administered prices reflect priorities and social needs as judged by central authorities; ultimately the criteria are political. Market prices reflect users' choices and producers' costs; ultimately the criteria are economic and technical. Administered prices frequently provide perverse incentives that lead to surpluses in some fields, shortages in others, wastage of resources, and deteriorating quality—the precise characteristics of the Soviet economy that few have described more starkly than Gorbachev himself. Market prices, including the prices of labor and capital, provide positive incentives that generally lead to equalization of supply and demand (rather than shortages and surpluses), improved product quality, and more efficient use of resources.

These points about price reform and its effects are familiar and widely accepted by such Soviet economists as Nikolai Shmelyev, Abel Aganbegyan, Vasili Selyunin, and others, no less than by economists in the West. The problem, and the disagreement, that

Published in the Los Angeles Times *with the title "Without Reform of Prices Soviet Economy Can't Rise" on September 8, 1989.*

85

arises at this point concerns "how to get there from here." Specifically, there is a worry that severe inflation would be unleashed by recourse to market-determined prices. This worry is based on a misunderstanding about the nature, causes, and symptoms of inflation, and its relation to price reform. And this misunderstanding, in turn, obscures a readily available remedy for the actual problems that rapid price reform would entail in a command economy like that of the Soviet Union.

Inflation arises when there is an increasing quantity of money seeking to buy a relatively fixed or reduced supply of goods, resulting in pervasive, sustained, and self-reinforcing price increases. Inflation comes in two versions: a "demand-pull" version, in which an increase in money supply creates a gap between monetary demand and the unchanged supply of goods and services, resulting in price increases across the board; and a "cost-push" version, in which nominal labor and other production costs begin to rise without a corresponding increase in productivity, and with an ensuing increase in the money supply to facilitate the initial cost increases. Once again, the result is pervasive and self-reinforcing price increases.

Neither of these conditions accurately describes the circumstances associated with price reform in the Soviet Union. Moving from administered toward market prices doesn't in itself imply or generate an increase in the money supply, or a diminished supply of goods, or a rise in production costs. Hence, inflation is not the real problem to be feared. In the transition from administered to market prices, the real problem lies elsewhere.

Under the existing system of administered prices combined with rationing of essential commodities, much of currently earned income simply cannot be spent because the supply of goods is deficient—both in quantity and quality. Hence, income that isn't spent accumulates as holdings of ruble cash or savings deposits. As a result, total holdings of cash and savings deposits are three or four times larger, in relation to Soviet GNP, than the corresponding holdings in the United States.

In some instances, accumulations held by individuals are extremely large, having been amassed over many years as a result not only of savings from legitimate income but also from various forms of underground or illegal economic activities. This presents a serious problem for an abrupt shift to market-determined prices, because these holdings could become active sources of monetary demand, boosting prices across the board, as well as resulting in major changes in relative prices among different commodities. While the supply of money would not have changed—so the formal ingredients of inflation would not be manifest—the existing money supply would turn over more frequently. In economic jargon, the "transaction velocity" of money would increase.

The concern this creates is that, with the ensuing rise in market prices, the existing supply of goods—especially consumer goods—would be commandeered by holders of cash or deposits, resulting in distributional inequities, labor unrest, and political stress to the system. To the extent this concern is warranted, an effective remedy is readily at hand—one that a command economy like that of the Soviet Union is singularly well-equipped to apply.

The remedy lies in an immediate reform of the monetary system: exchanging all large holdings (say, above 5,000 rubles) for long-term (say, 10 to 15 year) nontradable ruble bonds, and converting all small holdings of "old" rubles into "new" rubles. Such a monetary reform would enable price reform to succeed by sterilizing the bulk of the monetary overhang, allowing the market mechanism to determine relative commodity prices, and providing enterprises with clear signals as to where and when to increase, decrease, or terminate production.

Incidentally, this proposal carries no implication concerning the state's continued production and provision of "socially necessary" output. It simply means that production for the state would entail costs determined by market forces, would be purchased at market prices, and would be financed by taxes or other visible government revenues endorsed by the Congress of People's Deputies.

Perestroika's success need not wait for an indefinite future. It is readily at hand if the Soviet leadership makes use of the power of the state to move rapidly toward effective price reform. Those in the West who wish for this outcome might consider conditioning various forms of external help to the Soviets on aggressive movement by the leadership in this direction. Yet such conditionality may be unwise and counterproductive because it would appear to be demeaning and paternalistic. Besides, even without such conditions, Mr. Gorbachev and his supporters can do what needs to be done if they understand the problem and genuinely wish to resolve it.

Postaudit

The proposals to Mr. Gorbachev, and the advice to Western policymakers, are no less applicable currently than they were when the piece was written.

20

Soviet Economic Reform: Obstacles and Solutions

It is clear that the Soviet economy is in deep trouble. It is less clear how much of the trouble represents real decline during Gorbachev's 65 months in office, and how much reflects instead the increased visibility and audibility of conditions that existed before. Glasnost has made this distinction more difficult to discern: What was previously suppressed or obscured is now displayed and widely disseminated.

Statistics purporting to describe the Soviet economy are so unreliable that comparing currently observable conditions with those of the statistically recorded past is particularly suspect. A striking example is presented by a recent CIA/DIA report to the Joint Economic Committee, in which it was stated that the Soviet economy "stumbled badly" in 1989, although, according to the Agencies' questionable data, real per-capita consumption actually *rose* by 3.2 percent—a rate of growth well above that in the United States and Western Europe!

In any event, whether conditions have deteriorated sharply or only moderately from already low levels, the Soviet economy is sorely troubled and the need for drastic reform is compelling. So why, over more than five years in power, has Gorbachev moved forward so fitfully and ineffectively with genuine economic reform?

Several explanations are usually offered: (1) political opposition—the so-called "conservatives"—Ligachev, Polozkov, and their associates in the military and the KGB—remain strong and influential, despite their setbacks at the recent 28th Party Congress; (2) resistance and inertia in the party and government bureaucracy; (3) fears of

A slightly abbreviated version of this essay was published by the Los Angeles Times *under the title "Gorbachev: Part Problem, Part Solution" on September 12, 1990.*

strikes and unrest in the wake of the unemployment and inflation that might accompany thoroughgoing reform; and (4) strong pressure to maintain centralized control in order to meet and resolve the many conflicting sectoral demands for scarce resources.

But there is another major reason as well: Gorbachev himself! Notwithstanding his brilliance as a political tactician and his remarkable adroitness in political innovation, a fundamental question exists as to whether Gorbachev understands the kind of systemic reform that is required to reverse the economy's decline, and, if he does, whether he really favors moving in this direction?

It is a truism that all modern economies comprise a mixture of market-based and government-based roles and influences. Yet, to move the Soviet economy—as well as the economies of Eastern Europe—toward a balance between markets and governments that will be efficient, dynamic, and equitable, plainly requires an enormous expansion of the market's role and a corresponding diminution of the government's role.

To restructure the Soviet economy, as well as the economies of other "non-market economies," depends on articulating, explaining, enacting, and implementing a package of six mutually interacting sets of measures:

- *Monetary reform,* to ensure control of credit and the money supply.

- *Fiscal reform,* to assure budgetary balance, and to limit monetization of the budget deficit if one arises.

- *Price and wage reform,* to link prices with costs and demand, and wages with productivity.

- *Enterprise reform,* privatization, and legal protection of property rights, to provide incentives to workers and management that will accelerate supply responses in accord with changes in relative market prices.

- A *social security* "safety net" for those who may become unemployed as restructuring proceeds.

- *Currency convertibility,* to link the Soviet economy with the world economy and with competition in international markets.

These six components of systemic economic reform, which are prominent in the so-called Shatalin plan endorsed on September 11, 1990, by the Parliament of the Russian Republic and given a word of approval by Gorbachev himself, are mutually supporting and interactive. Each is less likely to work effectively without the reciprocal support of others on the list. Hence, efforts to "liberalize" the Soviet economy by piecemeal steps are more likely to founder than to succeed. For example, price and wage reform without monetary reform and fiscal restraint, and without privatization and enterprise reform, will generate inflation rather than competition and efficient production. And all of these, without the "safety net" provided by a social security system will create an anticipated fear of widespread unemployment. Finally, currency convertibility, to link the Soviet economy with international markets, depends on all of the foregoing measures if it is to work effectively.

Despite much press commentary to the contrary, Gorbachev has shown little ability or willingness to pursue such a comprehensive package of reform measures, and his public pronouncements suggest limited understanding of its systemic nature. Gorbachev has repeatedly asserted, for example, that he has no intention "to switch the country to capitalism" (most recently reiterated on June 21, 1990, at the Party Congress of the Russian Republic); that he wants to create a "regulated market economy"; and that he wants to preserve and invigorate socialism, not to supplant it. These pronouncements provide little ground for confidence in either his understanding of market systems or his intentions toward them.

To be sure, Gorbachev's remarkable capacity to shift ground and drastically change policy—and to do so with flair and conviction—should not be underestimated. He has amply demonstrated these qualities in the past in such different domains as the INF and START negotiations, German unification, and Germany's continued membership in NATO.

Nevertheless, a healthy degree of skepticism is still warranted that comprehensive economic reform will be enacted and implemented during Gorbachev's watch. It is as appropriate to view Gorbachev as part of the problem as it is to view him as the solution.

21

Tiananmen Square and Baku: Black and White . . . or Gray?

Returning from several weeks in China, one is bemused by realizing that major events, painted in black and white in the United States, appeared in Beijing as blurred shades of gray.

For example, chess champion Gary Kasparov appeared on Beijing's round-the-clock CNN channel at the end of January, reporting from Moscow on his evacuation from Baku, capital of Azerbaijan. While the Azerbaijanis were killing Armenians, he asserted, Soviet police and internal security forces stood idly by, failing to intercede as protectors of the beleaguered minority. Only *after* the Armenians had been killed, maimed, or evacuated, did the Soviet military intervene with tanks, APCs, and automatic weapons—in the process killing civilians and smashing buses with civilian passengers in them. The aim, Kasparov suggested, was to crush the Azerbaijani Popular Front—the republic's national independence movement.

Most of Kasparov's account was subsequently confirmed by other CNN reports received in Beijing and, indeed, a week later by Soviet Defense Minister Yazov, who explained the military action as necessary to restore law and order, and to suppress the planned takeover and separatist coup by the Azerbaijani nationalists. The army's aim was not to separate the Azeris from the Armenians and quell the bloody conflict between them, because that had been largely accomplished before the military intervened.

The account of events in Baku has striking similarities to, as well as differences from, the tragic events around Tiananmen Square in China in June 1989. Among the similarities:

A slightly abbreviated version of this essay was published by the Washington Times *under the title "Drawing a Line from Tiananmen to Baku" on March 23, 1990.*

- The types and extent of military force employed and the forcible imposition of martial law were simiiar in both instances.

- The declared purposes of these measures were the same in Tiananmen and Baku: to reestablish law and order and eliminate an actual or perceived threat to the existing regime—in China a threat to the Beijing regime's continuance, in Azerbaijan a threat of the republic's separation from the Soviet Union.

- Officially reported deaths inflicted by the army in Azerbaijan were somewhat over 100, with the military's own casualties reaching an additional 20 or 30; the officially reported Chinese casualty figures last June were not very different.

- Unofficial reports of civilian casualties in Azerbaijan ranged into the high hundreds, while in Beijing they ranged into the low thousands.

The differences, apart from the unofficial casualty figures already mentioned, include the following:

- An abundance of foreign correspondents and video cameras reported the violence from Beijing, while foreign correspondents were excluded from Nagorno-Karabakh and Baku in Azerbaijan. (From the standpoint of its effect on international perceptions, this may have been the most significant difference between the two tragedies.)

- Nationalists were the target of the military action in Azerbaijan, while students (as well as alleged "hooligans") were the victims in Tiananmen Square.

- A prior period of interethnic violence (between Armenians and Azeris) in Azerbaijan preceded the military intervention there, while largely peaceful demonstrations by students

had been under way for several months in Beijing before
the gross military intervention there.

• A severe clampdown on public criticism of government was
  enforced throughout China following the Tiananmen
  Square tragedy, while glasnost and widespread debate and
  criticism continued in the Soviet Union following the Baku
  violence.

All in all, the similarities are no less impressive than the differences between the two cases. Yet from the treatment in most of the
United States media as well as both public and official reactions, one
would infer that the Soviet leadership's actions were understandable
and acceptable, if not blameless, while those of the Chinese leadership
were egregious, brutal, and thoroughly discreditable.

In fact, the balance of credit and blame is much less clear. In both
instances—Tiananmen and Baku—ruthless escalation of violence was
employed to extinguish organized and growing opposition to the
establishment. Blatant military power, rather than political dialogue,
police pacification, and compromise, was the instrument chosen by
the State to preserve its position.

The reality is thus blurred and gray, rather than black and white.
The tragedy in China was not all black, nor was that in Azerbaijan all
white! Moreover, similar confrontations may occur in the future: for
example, in the Baltic states and southern republics of the Soviet
Union, and in the coastal provinces, Beijing, or Shanghai in China.
Both the Soviet Union (in the next several months) and China (in the
next few years) may face challenges that will once again require a
choice between using severe repressive force or accepting major
unwanted compromises to maintain state power.

II. Economic Issues and Policy

The Domestic Economic Debate

22

Why Economists Disagree

Economists and economics have never been as visible, audible, and publicized as they are now. Nor have the disagreements and divergent forecasts within the profession ever been as rife.

One consequence of this babble of prophesy is that the repute of economics and its practitioners has fallen to one of its lowest points in the 200 years since publication of the *Wealth of Nations*. The reason is simply that the testimony of professional economists is offered on almost any side of each major economic policy issue.

Was the Reagan tax program inflationary? "Yes," says Walter Heller; "no," says Milton Friedman; "not necessarily," says Murray Weidenbaum. How do high interest rates relate to inflation? "They contribute to it" (through indexing and cost of living adjustments), says economist X. "They're caused by it," says economist Y. "They result from efforts to control it" (through tighter monetary policy), says economist Z.

How will interest rates behave in the next year? Why did the dollar appreciate so sharply in the early 1980s, depreciate drastically in the mid- and late 1980s, and appreciate again in 1989? Will lower marginal tax rates and lower capital gains rates raise or reduce revenue?

On these and other key issues, the opinions of economists are spread as widely as forecasts of next month's weather.

As economists can be found on any side of these questions, the public has come to suspect that they are "hired guns"—whoever has a particular interest in espousing some economic policy can find some reputable economist to endorse it. It is one thing for lawyers to have

A slightly abbreviated version of this essay was published by Newsweek *on November 2, 1981.*

such a reputation, for lawyers are trained to be advocates, experts in organizing the best possible case for either side of an issue.

The analogy is admittedly imperfect. In general, *any* reputable lawyer can be found to defend almost any legally tenable position. The situation for economists is a bit different: it seems there's always *some* economist willing to back any side of most economic policy issues.

But economists are supposed to be scientists, schooled in seeking, testing, and finding "truth," and in acknowledging error when they encounter it. Even if their science is dismal, it's still supposed to be science.

Why then are their disagreements so sharp? There are four reasons:

- Economists use different benchmarks (often without spelling them out). When Brookings' economist George Perry asserts that Ronald Reagan's tax plan is inflationary, he is taking as his benchmark the Reagan expenditure budget already enacted by Congress. (The tax reductions are inflationary *given* that budget.) When Friedman and others rebut Perry, they're comparing Reagan's package of lower budget and lower taxes with the higher budget and higher taxes of Jimmy Carter's original program for fiscal year 1982—a different benchmark. (A deficit of specified size will have a smaller inflationary impact at a lower level of total government spending: the Reagan budget for 1982 involves a lower spending level than the Carter budget it replaced.)

- Economists often make different assumptions about the time period to which their conclusions apply. When Yale economist James Tobin asserts that lower tax rates will increase consumer spending, and macroeconomist Michael Evans contends instead that they will stimulate investment, each has a different period in mind: Tobin's is short-run, Evans' longer-run.

- Economists are usually reluctant to acknowledge the full extent of their ignorance. One of the great economists of an earlier age, Frank Knight, made a distinction between "risk" (knowing the odds), and "uncertainty" (not even knowing enough to calculate them). Ignorance is another name for this kind of uncertainty. And the plain fact is that economists share a degree of ignorance the extent of which they are understandably loath to admit.

We are on relatively solid ground in the domain of "microeconomics"—determination of prices in competitive or monopolistic markets, predicting the effects of minimum wages on employment, and so on. Our ignorance is formidable in the domain of macroeconomics: the interactions among monetary policy, tax policy, government spending, and government regulations in determining aggregate employment, savings, investment, and inflation. For all these effects depend on expectations: What is expected to occur will affect what does occur. If prices are expected to rise, consumer spending will tend to aggravate the rise, and vice versa. But the embarrassing truth is that we just don't know how expectations are determined: whether they're "adaptive," based on recent experience; or "rational," based not only on experience but also on estimates of how this experience will be altered as a result of expected government action or inaction and other relevant factors.

- Finally, economists have differing values and preferences. Just as there are deep ethical divisions among physicists and engineers over the development of new weapons systems, economists sometimes (often?) disagree on economic policies for reasons of pure (or impure) ideological preference. (Of course, to the extent that ignorance prevails, the room left for judgments based only on preferences is thereby enlarged.)

When John Galbraith decries cuts in minimum social security benefits or in student loans, he's probably motivated about equally by a distaste for the market's solutions (or a disbelief in their adequacy) and a predilection for government action to remedy them. When Friedman argues in favor of those cuts in government programs, his convictions are no doubt equally strong in the opposite direction: enthusiasm for the market's solutions, and distaste for the failures of meddlesome government. Moreover, these normative differences are no less real than those that lead Edward Teller to argue strongly for ballistic missile defense and Herbert York to argue with equal vehemence against it.

Recently, I had occasion to consult consecutively three orthopedic surgeons about a ligament injury. One recommended immediate surgery, the second suggested a cast for six weeks and then maybe surgery, and the third proposed rest and rehabilitation.

Perhaps economics doesn't look so bad if it's compared with medicine. Whether this should be viewed as ground for solace or grief is another question.

Postaudit

Some of the examples (the Reagan tax program), and some of the names (Walter Heller, Jim Tobin), have lost the pertinence or recognition they had in 1981. But the four reasons why economists often disagree, and the partly redemptive comparison between the diagnoses of doctors and economists, remain valid.

23

The Liberal-Conservative Switch

In case you haven't noticed, fully accredited "liberals" are now advocating policies and programs formerly espoused by equally anointed "conservatives," while conservatives have adopted positions formerly assumed by liberals. The switch has been confined to only a few specific issues—budget deficits, trade deficits, and protectionism. However, their importance and timeliness, when considered along with other confusing uses of the liberal-conservative labels, make this familiar terminology a semantic and political travesty. The term "liberal" is now about as appropriately applied to the conservative "right" as to the liberal "left."

Consider, for example, the issue that is the centerpiece of much recent liberal political rhetoric: namely, budget deficits. Citing a forecast by the Congressional Budget Office that federal deficits would rise from $178 billion in 1985 to $263 billion by 1989, Mr. Mondale characterized such deficits as "obscene." He concluded that drastic reductions in these deficits are the most compelling economic issue facing the country.

While the "conservative" Republican stance on this issue varies from more or less centrist Republicans to so-called radical ones, there is a common element to this diversity. The conservatives, whether relatively concerned about budget deficits (like Senator Dole), or relatively indifferent to them (like Congressman Kemp), typically evince a much more relaxed attitude toward the deficits than do liberals. For most liberals, eliminating budget deficits is the number one economic issue facing the country. For most conservatives, deficits, although not unimportant, rank well behind such issues as avoiding tax increases, curtailing the growth of government spending, and maintaining price stability.

A slightly abbreviated version of this essay was published under the title "Economic Labels—The Switch Is On" by the Los Angeles Times *on November 16, 1984.*

The contrast is striking when one recalls that not long ago the positions were exactly reversed. Then, conservatives viewed the federal deficit as a threat to the free enterprise system and a sign of the profligate expansion of government. Liberals, on the other hand, were either mildly or highly enthusiastic about deficits, rarely regarding them as a worry, and then only one of secondary or tertiary importance behind other, more compelling issues such as unemployment and the desirability of increasing government spending for both domestic and foreign policy purposes. Indeed, the New Deal, the Fair Deal, and the Great Society—which provide the philosophical underpinnings of the liberal approach to government—were predicated on the acceptability if not desirability of sustained budget deficits.

Criticism of U.S. trade deficits by liberals has been only slightly less vehement than that of budget deficits. Because liberals typically view the trade deficit as representing an export of jobs abroad and a loss of jobs at home, they have become strong advocates for protection of the U.S. market against "excessive" or "unfair" foreign competition.

It is true that the conservatives' recent record on free trade has been mixed: For example, the Reagan Administration rejected import quotas for copper but accepted higher tariffs on Japanese motorcycles. Nevertheless, as between the two groups, liberal Democrats are now more staunchly protectionist than conservative Republicans. For example, Mr. Mondale advocated rigid quotas to reduce imported steel from an existing 25 percent share of the U.S. market to no more than 17 percent. By contrast, the Reagan Administration opposed steel quotas, and instead favored voluntary "restraint" by exporters to limit their share of the U.S. market to no more than 25 percent.

In sum, conservatives—whose lineage traces back to the notoriously protective Smoot-Hawley Tariff Act of 1929—now urge relatively liberal trade policies, while liberals—whose lineage traces back to GATT and to generalized reductions in international trade barriers—now advocate relatively severe forms of protection.

A similar switch in the meaning of the liberal-conservative labels arises in another context: namely, in discussions of economic reforms in foreign countries. For example, the Central Committee of the Chinese Communist Party approved in 1984 an extraordinary economic plan endorsing free market incentives, flexible prices, income and wage differentials based on productivity, and the ending of subsidies for more than a million state enterprises. According to the *Wall Street Journal*, a diplomat from one socialist-led government of Western Europe characterized this remarkable plan as "much more liberal [sic] than I had expected."

Use of the term "liberal" to describe such reforms in China, as well as their counterpart and antecedent in Hungary's "market socialism," is now a generally accepted practice. "Liberalization" is also a familiar way of characterizing similar measures favored by the socialist government of France, and by the relatively few successful developing countries (such as Korea, Taiwan, Malaysia, Hong Kong, and Singapore) that have long since adopted such policies.

The common core of such liberalizing reforms lies, of course, in the relative emphasis they accord to reliance on the free market rather than on government in the allocation of economic resources. This use of the term "liberal" derives from the fact that all of these reforms can be traced to the common intellectual legacy of so-called liberal or neoclassical economics. But this is the same legacy that constitutes the core of three Reagan Administration's conservative economic policies: namely, reduced government intervention in the free market; strengthened incentives for private investment, work, and saving; and greater reliance on competition.

There is an oxymoronic quality to all of this: What is liberal in China and Hungary, or even in France and the developing countries, is conservative in the United States! Once again, we encounter the liberal-conservative switch, and once again the semantic travesty of the standard labels.

Discussion in the media and elsewhere would be much clearer if it referred simply to the relative reliance to be placed on markets or on governments, and consigned the overused liberal and conservative labels to the shelf for a long rest period.

Postaudit

The revolutions of 1989 in Central and Eastern Europe reinforce the theme of this piece: liberals in these countries favor free markets, property rights, privatization of state enterprises, and sharply reduced government regulation. Conservatives, including anticommunists as well as reform communists, resist marketizing reforms and favor a greater degree of central planning. And in the United States,

Democratic liberals tend by and large to be more protectionist—especially concerning the Japanese—than Republican conservatives!

24

The Hazards of
Economic Forecasting

As we absorb the daily barrage of predictions about outyear budget and trade deficits, higher interest rates, economic "overheating," and resumed inflation, prudence suggests we should ask three general questions about economic forecasts: How reliable are they? Why? And what should be done about them?

The answer to the first question is: "Not very." Consider a few examples:

- At the start of 1983, both supply-side and Keynesian forecasting models predicted only modest economic growth in the United States for the ensuing year. The Council of Economic Advisors' initial growth forecast for 1983 was between 1.5 and 2 percent, while the forecasts of the Congressional Budget Office, Data Resources, Inc., Wharton, Chase, and a number of others were half again larger. In fact, the actual 1983 rate was over 6 percent! The actual record was thus more than double the consensus of the principal forecasters.

- In July 1983, after three quarters of the fiscal year had elapsed, the Reagan Administration's own forecast of the expected budget deficit for the entire fiscal year 1983 was $212 billion. Three months later, the actual deficit turned out to be only $195 billion, an error of 8 percent. For fiscal year 1984, the Administration has forecast a deficit of $179

A slightly abbreviated version of this essay was published under the title "Pin a Tail on the Forecasts" by the New York Times on June 30, 1984.

billion. But, according to some estimates by nongovernment forecasters made in April after two quarters had elapsed, the deficit is likely to be only $162 billion—at least 9 percent less than the government's own forecast.

- In March 1984, the Department of Commerce's "flash" estimate of the first quarter's real GNP growth rate was 7.2 percent. By the middle of May, the actual rate turned out to be 8.8 percent, a 22 percent error.

The examples are illustrative, not exhaustive. They could be multiplied many times.

Why are forecasts so frequently wide of the mark? The principal reason is ignorance rather than partisanship. The errors are not confined to forecasters of one policy persuasion or another. They are made by supply siders and Keynesians, by both government and business forecasters, by academics and research firms, by Republicans and Democrats. Forecasting errors are made on all sides of the policy spectrum simply because economists are much less knowledgeable about macroeconomics than about microeconomics. Indeed, while economists mainly talk about macroeconomics, what they really know about is microeconomics.

The answer to the third question ("What to do about the forecasts?") is a combination of piety and common sense. The common sense is that economic forecasts should be taken with plenty of seasoning: not ignored, but certainly not taken too seriously. This caution is especially warranted for forecasts that are in the distant future. The more distant is the forecast, the less reliable it's likely to be. "Distance" here means a year or even less, as the preceding examples suggest.

The piety is that the forecasts should be improved. Improving them depends fundamentally on replacing macroeconomic ignorance with macroeconomic knowledge. This is bound to be a difficult and slow process for reasons that are both familiar and enduring. However, while this process proceeds at its inevitably glacial pace, two simple improvements could be made easily and quickly.

The first improvement would be to have forecasts presented not as *point* estimates (for example, it was absurd for the Treasury to forecast a 1983 federal budget deficit of exactly $195.4 billion), but instead as a *range*, together with an indication of the probabilities associated with several different parts of the range. In other words, economic forecasts should be expressed in a form that conveys at least as much information about the true uncertainty of the estimates as is conveyed in standard weather predictions. For example, "overcast and cooler with a 40 percent chance of showers" might be paralleled by a prediction of the following sort: "GNP growth rate of 5 percent, with a 50 percent chance that the rate will be 2 percent lower." This is easy to do with current computerized macroeconomic models. One reason the forecasts are so rarely presented this way is because the modelers are reluctant to highlight the real uncertainty surrounding their forecasts. Users of the forecasts should insist that this reluctance be overcome.

A second improvement would be to keep a box score, or "batting average," for each of the principal forecasters, as a regular, continuing, and readily accessible record.[1] For example, six indicators could be tabulated for each major forecaster's annual predictions: (1) GNP growth; (2) the inflation rate (that is, the change in GNP deflator, or in the producer price index, or in the consumer price index); (3) the year-end level of employment (a much more reliable statistic than the unemployment rate); (4) the federal budget deficit for the year as a whole; (5) the year-end prime rate of interest; and (6) the year-end exchange rate of the dollar (say, relative to the yen, the mark, or the European Currency Unit). To keep the system simple, one point could be assigned to each forecast that is no more than 5 percent above or below the actual value at the end of the year, with prorated reductions in score tied to the degree of inaccuracy of the forecast. Six would be a perfect score.

Who would keep score? Candidates with a possible institutional interest as well as the necessary competence include the National Bureau of Economic Research, the Department of Commerce, the Brookings Institution, the American Enterprise Institute, the *Wall Street Journal*, the *New York Times*, the *Los Angeles Times*, or even The RAND Corporation.

A simple innovation of this sort would help to inform the unwary public about the best and the worst, as well as about how bad even the best are. It would also tend, over time, to improve the forecasts them-

---

[1] The following chapter develops and applies a system for scoring several of the principal forecasters for the 1983 to 1986 period.

selves. As Samuel Johnson once observed, "when a man knows he is to be hanged in a fortnight, it concentrates his mind wonderfully." So too the prospect of having one's score duly registered at the end of each year would make the forecasters more accountable and more responsible. Over a period of several years, the market would be likely to assure that the better ones survive and the others would succumb. Hence, the prevailing forecasts would be improved.

Postaudit

Aside from the somewhat ancient (1983, 1984) data that are cited, the proposed answers to the three initial questions are equally valid today. Although the recent numbers are different, forecasts are no more reliable currently than in the earlier period referred to in the article. For example, the consensus forecast made in early January 1990 for annualized real GNP growth in the first quarter of the year was 1 percent. The result for the quarter was 2.5 percent—an error of 150 percent! As one prominent forecaster recently observed: "I don't usually make a habit of comparing what I said at the beginning of the quarter with what I say at the end. It would just depress me!"

I made a preliminary effort to implement the idea of a scoring system for forecasters (see the following chapter). It remains to be placed on a regular basis—like the baseball batting averages that are its analogue.

25

Scoring the Economic Forecasters

The Setting

Economic forecasting has something in common with earthquake prediction and medical diagnostics. The phenomena are complex and imperfectly understood. The stakes are high. Enormous datasets have been collected, although questions frequently arise about their reliability.

Also, in all three instances the explanatory theory that exists is inexact and fluid. The imprecision of earthquake prediction theory was evident in the strikingly different interpretations placed upon the series of sharp temblors in Southern California in July 1986. According to the mutually inconsistent predictions inferred from these events, a major earthquake is more likely to occur in the near term because the recent temblors were an indicator of what's in store; less likely because the previously existing tectonic stresses have now been relieved; or neither more nor less likely than before because nothing fundamental was changed by the 1986 quakes!

The three domains are also alike in that their respective practitioners often argue that any particular case immediately at hand—for example, the economy's behavior next year or last year, or the prognosis for a particular patient, or the outlook for earthquakes in California in the next year or ten—is unique, "a class of one," and hence no generalization or prediction can be made without so many qualifications as to depreciate its meaning.

Finally, the three are alike in that no systematic method exists for regularly tracking practitioners in the way that, say, major league batters or pitchers can be tracked from year to year. Hence, in the absence of either a metric or an institutional memory, users are unable to distinguish the more accurate forecasters from those who are less so.

Published in the Public Interest, *Number 88, Summer 1987.*

In the apt words of Charles Morris, "the rules for modern forecasting are to do it cheekily and frequently, to insist on the solidity of each new forecast, and to count on the general lack of interest in the subject to obscure yesterday's bumblings."

Something would surely be gained by having a standard scoring system to distinguish the heavy hitters from the whiffers. Such a scorecard would help to inform the unwary public about the best and the worst, as well as about how bad even the best are. It would also tend, over time, to improve forecasting. As Samuel Johnson once observed, "when a man knows he is to be hanged in a fortnight, it concentrates his mind wonderfully." So too would the prospect of having one's score publicized. Over several years, the market would assure that the better forecasters survive and that the others would find another line of work.

Putting the Forecasters in the Batter's Box

To accomplish these aims, a fairly straightforward, intuitively plausible method has been devised. The method, which I have called the Economic Forecast Scoring System (EFSS), expresses the absolute difference between forecast and outcome as a percentage of the actual outcome: The larger the percentage, the bigger the forecast error. Thus, a perfectly accurate forecast would have a zero score, while a score of one would imply the forecast erred by 100 percent. The latter might be construed as equivalent to a strikeout for a baseball batter, although theoretically EFSS allows practitioners to err by even larger percentages. (Actually, strikeouts occur very rarely in the component forecasts discussed and scored below: for example, only in such cases as the inflation rate forecasts made in 1983 and 1986, when the *average* forecast errors were nearly 100 percent, and some individual forecasters exceeded the average by a wide margin.)

In EFSS, only the *absolute* difference between forecast and outcome matters in calculating the percentage error; whether the forecast is above or below the outcome doesn't affect the score. Thus, a forecast of the real GNP growth rate that diverges from the actual year-over-year growth by a given amount scores equally under EFSS, regardless of whether the divergence exceeds or falls short of the realized growth.

Of course, other scoring rules, with somewhat different merits and demerits, might be devised. For example, the scores could be based on the absolute errors alone, rather than the percentage of the outcome represented by these errors. Or the errors might be scaled according to the variability of the outcome rather than its level. EFSS uses percentage error as a scoring metric because it is salient and easily understood, rather than because it is unexceptionable.

For EFSS to be applied fairly, the forecasts must have been made at the same point in time prior to the outcome that is forecast. It is also evident that comparison among the forecasters requires that their scores be tracked repeatedly, across several time periods.

Four economic indicators have been chosen for EFSS: real GNP growth on a year-over-year basis; average change in the consumer price index; the three-month treasury bill rate averaged over the year; and the rate of unemployment averaged over the year.

These four indicators were selected because they are among the most significant macroeconomic guideposts for the economy as a whole, and because yearly forecasts for these indicators are readily available on a comparable basis for most of the prominent forecasters, including those associated with the federal government. In principle, several additional indicators no less important than the selected ones would have been worthwhile to include—notably, the federal budget deficit, the trade or current account deficit or surplus, the dollar's exchange rate, and the total level of employment (which is a much more accurate figure than the rate of unemployment). Unfortunately, these indicators are not covered on a comparable basis by most of the forecasters. Still other, more narrowly focused indicators (for example, before-tax and after-tax profits, industrial production, and housing starts) that might be of particular interest to some forecast users, are omitted from this initial scoring venture to keep it relatively simple.

The four indicators have been used in scoring fifteen of the best-known forecasters, including two from government (the Congressional Budget Office and the Office of Management and Budget) and thirteen from private firms: the Bank of America, Chase Econometrics, Data Resources, Dean Witter, Du Pont, Evans Economics, *Fortune*, Manufacturers Hanover, Merrill Lynch Economics, Morgan Guaranty, Pennzoil, Wharton Econometrics, and the Blue Chip Consensus Forecast.

The scores cover forecasts for the four years 1983 to 1986. All of the forecasts, except for those of CBO, were made in January of the year under consideration; for example, the year-over-year GNP growth forecasts for 1983 were made in January 1983.[1] The CBO forecasts were made in February of each corresponding year. Outcome measures are taken from *Economic Indicators*, prepared for the Joint Economic Committee by the Council of Economic Advisers.

The 1983 to 1986 period included several dramatic changes in the external economic environment—the collapse of oil prices, and the extraordinarily high rise (1983 to 1985) and then sharp fall (1986) in the dollar's exchange value—which might have resulted in unusually large forecast errors in other economic indicators. However, all of the forecasters were subject to this same jeopardy. Consequently, while their collective performance as a group might be adversely affected, their *relative* scores would not be. To be sure, if a particular forecaster happened to be lucky in anticipating one of these discontinuities, his relative performance would be improved. However, the resulting boost in performance would only be temporary. If, on the other hand, a particular forecaster is unusually and recurringly good at anticipating such apparent discontinuities, then skill is probably a better explanation than luck.

Moreover, it's not entirely clear that the 1983 to 1986 period really did display a greater profusion of discontinuities than is normal. For example, consider the closing of the gold window and the imposition of price controls in 1971, or the quadrupling of oil prices in 1973 to 1974 and their doubling again in 1979 to 1980. Economic forecasting is just a difficult line of work in almost any time period!

How Did They Score?

Table 25.1 shows the annual EFSS scores (in parentheses) and the corresponding rankings for the fifteen forecasters for the four economic indicators (GNP growth, CPI change, T-bill rate, and unemployment rate), for each of the four years from 1983 to 1986. Column five of the table shows the composite scores and the relative

---

[1] In the very few instances where one of the indicators was missing from a forecaster's predictions, the missing score was assumed to be equal to the average of the other forecasters' scores for that indicator in that year.

Table 25.1.
Forecasters' Scores and Rankings, 1983-1986[a]

Forecaster	1983 Rank Score	1984 Rank Score	1985 Rank Score	1986 Rank Score	Composite Rank Score 1983-1986
Bank of America	14 (1.379)	12 (0.551)	5 (0.444)	8 (1.434)	10 (3.708)
Chase Econometrics	9 (1.199)	8 (0.502)	13 (0.696)	3 (1.006)	6 (3.403)
Data Resources	13 (1.335)	1 (0.350)	1 (0.143)	4 (1.070)	1 (2.898)
Dean Witter	2 (0.923)	13 (0.555)	15 (0.874)	12 (1.717)	12 (4.069)
Du Pont	1 (0.918)	9 (0.515)	9 (0.608)	2 (0.999)	3 (3.040)
Evans Economics	15 (1.570)	7 (0.494)	3 (0.256)	14 (2.014)	13 (4.334)
Fortune	3 (0.960)	11 (0.541)	11 (0.646)	11 (1.595)	11 (3.742)
Manufacturers Hanover	11 (1.275)	5 (0.483)	2 (0.150)	10 (1.543)	7 (3.451)
Merrill Lynch	6 (1.117)	14 (0.557)	8 (0.602)	5 (1.210)	8 (3.486)
Morgan Guaranty	10 (1.213)	3 (0.401)	6 (0.466)	7 (1.249)	5 (3.329)
Pennzoil	8 (1.172)	10 (0.538)	14 (0.730)	13 (2.008)	14 (4.448)
Wharton	5 (1.098)	4 (0.408)	10 (0.625)	1 (0.799)	2 (2.930)
Blue Chip Consensus	4 (1.047)	6 (0.490)	7 (0.536)	9 (1.495)	9 (3.568)
OMB	12 (1.332)	15 (0.958)	12 (0.691)	15 (2.457)	15 (5.438)
CBO	7 (1.136)	2 (0.385)	4 (0.362)	6 (1.245)	4 (3.128)

[a]Columns one to four show EFSS scores in parentheses that represent the unweighted sum of the separate forecast errors expressed as percentages of actual GNP growth, CPI change, T-bill rate, and unemployment rate in each of the four years, 1983-1986. If a forecaster did not publish a forecast for one of the indicators in a particular year, I assumed the missing observation was equal to the average of the remaining forecasts for that indicator in that year. T-bill forecasts by the Bank of America were not originally published outside the bank and would not, in any event, have been appropriate to use because their probabilistic structure made them noncomparable to the other forecasts in the sample. The composite EFSS score in column five is the sum of the individual four-year scores. Scores and rankings in the table have been slightly revised from a similar table published in the *Wall Street Journal* on June 10, 1987, to correct for a reporting error in earlier data.

rankings of the fifteen forecasters based on the sum of their annual EFSS scores over the period.

Interpretation of the annual EFSS scores is straightforward: for example, the Bank of America score of 1.379 in 1983 (column one of Table 25.1) signifies that the bank's forecasts in that year erred by a total of 137.9 percent spread over the four economic indicators included in the scoring system. The total score shown in the table doesn't indicate how the aggregate error was divided among the four indicators. (Actually, in the cited example nearly all of the 137.9 percent resulted from errors in forecasting GNP growth and the CPI increase.)

In adding the separate unweighted scores for the four economic indicators to arrive at each year's aggregate EFSS score, I am implicitly assuming that they are of equal importance, and am also making no allowance for possible differences in the difficulty of forecasting each indicator.

The assumption of equal weights among the four indicators is more transparent, even if no less arbitrary, than would be the assignment of differential weights (say, treating GNP growth as twice as important as each of the other indicators). Of course, an individual forecast user may be much more interested in one of the indicators than in the others. For example, a firm with typically large short-term borrowing requirements might be most interested in the treasury bill rate, and therefore might wish to assign a heavier weight to this component in arriving at a total score.

The four indicators evidently differ in the degree of difficulty involved in forecasting them, although EFSS makes no allowance for this difference. If we use as a measure of forecasting difficulty the average error experienced by the fifteen forecasters as a group, it appears that the CPI change and GNP growth are the hardest to forecast, the T-bill rate is next, and the unemployment rate is the easiest of the four, as shown in Table 25.2.

In part, the difference in forecast difficulty, as reflected by the average errors shown in Table 25.2, is simply due to the greater year-to-year volatility of GNP growth and CPI changes, and the greater year-to-year stability of the T-bill and unemployment rates. But only in part: Actually, the CPI changes showed relatively less variability over the 1983 to 1986 period than the GNP growth rate, yet the fifteen forecasters had more trouble in forecasting the CPI than the GNP.

Table 25.2
Average Forecast Errors for Component Indicators,
1983–1986[a]
(In percentage)

	GNP Growth	CPI Change	T-Bill Rate	Unemployment
1983	44.3	49.8	13.6	10.1
1984	19.4	20.7	10.0	7.8
1985	24.4	13.3	11.4	3.1
1986	25.3	98.6	19.3	2.4

[a]Percentages are the average errors realized by the fifteen forecasters included in the sample.

Although the different average errors suggest differences in the difficulty of forecasting the four indicators, it is worth noting that the fifteen forecasters display very considerable variation from these average errors in their individual forecasts. Thus, the deviations from the average errors shown in Table 25.2 are substantial among the fifteen forecasters, whether or not the average errors are large or small! The implication of this point is that the individual forecasters are much more "independent" of one another than might have been expected.

Forecasters, Forecasting, and the Wary Consumer

As the EFSS results summarized in Table 25.1 plainly indicate, all of the forecasters are inaccurate some of the time, and some are inaccurate most of the time. The composite scores and rankings for the 1983 to 1986 period (column five of Table 25.1) suggest that the fifteen forecasters cluster in three groups, which are separated by discernible gaps or "knees" between them: a group of four relatively "heavy-hitters," including DRI, Wharton, Du Pont, and CBO; a middle group covering the fifth- through the tenth-ranked forecasters, including Morgan, Chase, Manufacturers Hanover, Merrill Lynch, the Blue Chip Consensus, and *Fortune*; and a lower tier of the lightest hitters, including Evans, Dean Witter, Pennzoil, Bank of America, and OMB.

Notwithstanding these gradations, the relative standings of the forecasters vary widely from year to year. Although Bank of America ranked near the bottom over the four-year period, it was one of the best in 1985. Dean Witter had the second most accurate forecast of the entire group in 1983, but was the least accurate in 1985. Evans was third from the top in 1985, but fourteenth in 1986. DRI was near the bottom in 1983, and at or near the top in 1984, 1985, and 1986. Among the heavy hitters, CBO is the most consistent. In general, a particular forecaster's standing in a particular year doesn't tell a lot about its relative performance in a subsequent year.

Considering the fifteen forecasters as a group, their relative rankings in 1983, as they appear in Table 25.1, are not significantly correlated with those in 1984. Although the rank correlation between 1984 and 1985 is statistically significant, that between 1985 and 1986 is not. The degree of association (concordance) among the rankings over the four-year period as a whole is so small (.195) that one cannot reject the hypothesis that the separate four-year rankings among the forecasters are unrelated.

Conclusions

These results make explicitly and quantitatively clear what is impressionistically and qualitatively already well known: macro-economic forecasting is a hazardous, difficult, and imperfect art. There are better and worse performers according to the EFSS scores, but the best is none too good. GNP and CPI changes are evidently harder to forecast, as reflected by their average forecast errors, than the T-bill rate and unemployment. Yet the variability around these average errors is substantial, suggesting that the forecasters practice their art more independently than might have been supposed. If they share a general proneness to err, they also display a proclivity to make their own individual errors as well.

It is reasonable to conclude that a lot of room remains for improvements in forecasting. But how much improvement can be made and how quickly is open to question, both because of the enormous and growing complexity of the economic system and the changeability of the relationships within it.

Lest macroeconomic forecasts and forecasters be judged too hastily, it's worth noting that they appear in a much more favorable light when compared with forecasts in other fields that are concerned with much narrower and presumably simpler phenomena than the behavior of the economy as a whole. After all, it was only a few years ago that experts made forecasts of an impending teacher surplus and a doctor shortage, whereas current conditions in both fields—at prevailing compensation rates—are now proclaimed to be exactly the opposite of the forecasts. And it is easy to forget that four or five years ago the consensus forecast of oil prices in the mid-1980s was more than twice the price levels that eventuated.

In the domain of macroeconomic forecasting, caveat emptor is a warranted, if perhaps gratuitous, admonition. However, closer adherence to it can, with the help provided by EFSS, have at least two salutary effects: contributing to more flexible and effective business planning by increasing awareness of the real uncertainties that are involved in underlying macroeconomic assumptions; and, by the process of Darwinian selection, contributing to improving the practice of economic forecasting. EFSS can also help to distinguish economic forecasting from earthquake prediction and medical diagnostics by providing consumers with means of calibrating practitioners in the field.

Postaudit

EFSS was designed and intended to be a regularized, repetitive, and recurring device to improve public information about the accuracy of forecasts and to stimulate forecasters to do better. These goals seem to me no less worthy now than they were then. That I haven't repeated and sustained the exercise is due to limitations of time rather than second thoughts about the concept's merit.

26

A Proper Perspective on the Twin Deficits

While it's true that the deficit twins—the budget deficit and the trade deficit—are important, the degree of concern currently being expressed about them is exaggerated. Failure to reduce, let alone eliminate, the deficits may be imprudent. It would not be a disaster.

Moreover, focusing on the deficits diverts attention from the economy's more significant longer-run problem: namely, the aggregate savings rate. Were the deficit problems to be eased while the savings rate remained low, U.S. economic prospects would be bleak. On the other hand, if the savings rate were raised by 2 or 3 percent of the GNP, the longer-term economic outlook would be sanguine whether or not the deficits remained.

To help focus on what's primary and what's secondary, it is worth recalling a few fundamentals about the deficit twins, the relation between them, and their consanguine parentage.

The trade deficit—or to be more accurate, the current account deficit—is definitionally equal to the difference between savings and investment. In an accounting sense, the amount by which investment exceeds savings is exactly equal to the amount by which imports of goods and services exceeds exports.

In the past decade, the aggregate U.S. savings rate has declined by about 3 or 4 percent (from about 16 or 17 percent of the GNP to about 13 percent),[1] while aggregate investment has remained at about 17

A slightly abbreviated version of this essay was published under the title "In Hearing Deficit Alarms, We Turn a Deaf Ear to Some Positive Points" in the Los Angeles Times *on February 6, 1989. The full text was presented in testimony to the Senate Budget Committee on February 22, 1989.*

[1] One of the standard, but seriously misleading, practices in the sometimes polemical writing on this matter is to calculate the U.S. savings rate as *net* savings expressed as

percent. This 3 or 4 percent difference has been reflected in the current account deficit. To reduce or eliminate the current account deficit implies a reduction in investment, an increase in savings, or a combination of the two. Among these three alternatives, the first is less preferred than either of the other two, as well as less preferred than continuation of the deficit.

While the precise determinants of the savings rate, as well as its accurate measurement, are imperfectly understood as well as controversial, the government budget is clearly one of the important influences on aggregate savings. This follows from the accounting identity that gross savings represent the difference between gross national product and the *sum* of private consumption spending and government spending on goods and services. Thus, at a given GNP level, gross savings are reduced by either higher consumption or higher government spending. Government purchases of goods and services reduce aggregate savings *whether the government spending is financed by taxes or by borrowing*. The variable that matters is the *magnitude* of government spending; how it is financed is of secondary importance in its effect on savings. To the extent that taxes reduce savings, and government borrowing reduces private consumption spending (the so-called "Ricardian effect"), the size of the federal budget deficit is of secondary importance, while the size of government spending is of primary importance in its effect on savings.

Of course, there are good reasons for wanting to see the federal budget deficit reduced: for example, to keep interest rates down, to damp inflationary expectations, to restore fiscal policy as a credible instrument for countering recessions, and finally, to convey—internationally as well as domestically—the image of a responsible government that lives within its means. While acknowledging that

---

a fraction of *gross* national product, thereby shrinking the rate by 9 or 10 percent. This practice is both bad accounting and bad economics: bad accounting because depreciation charges should not be left out of the numerator if they are included in the denominator; and bad economics because a relatively large proportion of U.S. plant modernization, as well as the technological advancement embodied in new equipment, is accomplished through capital consumption allowances and depreciation charges, which are nontaxable business expenses. Those who are guilty of this practice include many people who should know better, and some who do.

point, it's worth adding a few heterodoxical words to clarify, as well as extenuate, the effects of the federal budget deficit.

First, from the standpoint of the effects of budget deficits on credit markets and the international accounts, what matters is the consolidated budgets of the states as well as the federal government, not the federal budget alone. Because the states have amassed a substantial aggregate budget surplus in recent years, the consolidated deficit shrinks by $50 to $60 billion. Thus, the consolidated budget deficit that results for the current year is $100 billion, or about 2 percent of the U.S. GNP—a figure not out of line with comparable figures in Japan, West Germany, or the United Kingdom.

Second, the federal budget deficit exercises a braking effect on the otherwise strong political pressures in a pluralistic democracy for government spending to rise. In general, there is a small negative, but statistically significant, relationship between the size of the federal deficit in one year and the increase in federal spending in the succeeding year, net of inflation and net of debt service.

Finally, as Robert Eisner has demonstrated, there's a substantial component of capital formation in federal government spending. Eisner has estimated this component at between $100 and $250 billion annually—the higher figure depends on whether military procurement and military R&D are included. It is not inappropriate to finance genuine and productive public infrastructure by government borrowing, because this infrastructure contributes to improved functioning of the economy and to widening the tax base, provided the capital expenditures have been wisely selected in the first place.

Turning to the other twin, there are encouraging signs that the trade deficit is already diminishing under the impact of two powerful market forces: the lowered exchange value of the dollar, and the discipline imposed on U.S. producers by having to compete for market share with foreign imports in the United States, and with foreign products in world export markets. As a result, the trade deficit in 1988 is likely to be about $137 billion—more than $30 billion below the $170 billion deficit of 1987. The 1988 figure will probably decrease further in 1989 by another $20 or $30 billion.

As the U.S. trade deficit declines, the adjustment problem this will create for the rest of the world will probably be considerably greater than that for the U.S. economy. It is too easy for our friends in Western Europe and East Asia to forget that, for the U.S. trade deficit to diminish, the trade surpluses of other countries—especially Japan, West Germany, and the newly industrialized Asian countries—will have to decline; or they and other countries will have to experience trade deficits; or some combination of the two will have to occur. One finds much more criticism these days from European and Asian governments concerning the need for the United States to "do something about its trade deficit" than recognition of what this implies for their own economies![2]   And these implications remain whether the U.S. trade deficit is reduced by actions that affect the U.S. budget deficit, the U.S. savings rate, or U.S. investment.

This prospect could be adversely affected by one development that has generally been overlooked.   The attractiveness of U.S. assets, including real property, to foreign investors may propel a continued strong desire by foreigners to invest in the United States, in the process raising the dollar's value and impeding the downward adjustment of the U.S. trade deficit.   It is worth bearing in mind that capital flows can *generate* a trade deficit, rather than being generated by it.

In sum, neither deficit warrants alarm.   The federal budget and the trade accounts are less significant indicators of the economy's health than are the maintenance of sustained real economic growth, high employment, and low inflation.

Postaudit

The content and conclusion of the article remain valid.   The U.S. trade deficit in 1989 was $20 billion less than that of 1988, and the federal budget deficit declined by about $15 billion in 1989 from the 1988 level.   My 1988 estimates were accurate.   Economic growth, high employment, and reasonable price stability are the proper goals of macroeconomic policy; reducing the deficits is of secondary importance.

---

[2] For example, by the end of the 1990s Japan should become a "mature" creditor nation—earning more from its prior foreign investments than it is paying out in new investments, implying that it will be importing more than it is exporting.

27

Public Deficits and Private Savings

Public budget deficits are too high and should be reduced. Private savings are too low and should be increased. The presidential candidates and the party platforms agree on the first proposition; their disagreement relates only to the means to be used and the urgency of using them. Where the candidates stand on the second proposition can only be surmised because, while devoting ample if not excessive verbiage to the first proposition, they have scarcely addressed the second.

This omission is noteworthy because the two issues are not only related but the savings issue is more important. The two issues are related because private savings provide a cushion for public deficits: The private sector is obliged to spend less than its after-tax earnings to enable the public sector to spend more than its tax receipts.

Yet the savings issue is more important than the deficit issue in three fundamental respects. First, if private savings were higher, deficits would be less troublesome—perhaps they would even be tolerable—and interest rates would be lower. (Moreover, the size of the deficit would be reduced because each percentage point reduction in interest rates that would result from higher savings would lower by about $12 billion the annual budget costs of carrying the nation's $1.5 trillion debt.) Second, if deficits are reduced not by lowering government spending, but instead by increasing taxes, the effect of which is to decrease private savings, the economy's predicament may be as bad with the lower deficit as it was with the higher one.

Finally, if U.S. savings rates continue to be as low as they've been, let alone decline further, the American economy will have serious downstream problems of sustaining investment, productivity growth, innovation, and international competitiveness, *regardless of what happens to the deficit.*

A slightly abbreviated version of this essay was published under the title "Our Problem Isn't So Much Borrowing" by the Wall Street Journal *on September 28, 1984.*

Thus, the savings rate is a serious problem quite apart from the budget deficit, whereas the deficit is a more or less serious problem depending on whether the savings rate is, respectively, low or high.

Since 1970, U.S. gross private saving (which includes personal saving, undistributed corporate profits, and capital consumption allowances) has varied between about 13 to 17 percent of GNP; probably the actual variation has been greater than the estimate. Lest this 4 percent variation be dismissed as insignificant, it should be noted that, at current GNP levels, it represents over $200 billion, more than a third above the federal budget deficit of 1989.[1]

Apart from its limited, though not negligible, variability, the U.S. gross savings rate is appreciably lower than that of certain other major industrial countries (Japan's rate is 27 percent and Germany's 21 percent), although comparable to that of others (the savings rate in the United Kingdom and Sweden is 16 percent).

Personal saving in the United States—which is typically between a quarter and a third of gross private saving—has shown a sharper and more puzzling variation than the gross rate, declining from 8.6 percent of disposable personal income in 1973 to only 5 percent by 1983. The fluctuating but generally downward trend in the intervening years is shown in Figure 27.1. As the figure indicates, the U.S. personal savings rate declined by 28 percent from 1981 to 1983 (from 6.9 to 5 percent).

The ten-year decline in the U.S. savings rate is all the more extraordinary because it occurred during a period when real per-capita disposable personal income rose by 15 percent! Richer individuals and families usually save more than poorer ones, so increased per-capita income would generally be expected to lead to higher rather than lower savings rates.

Neither demand-side (Keynesian) nor supply-side economics provides a satisfactory explanation for the puzzling pattern of U.S. savings. Keynesian economics has usually assumed that aggregate savings rates are fixed, when in fact they vary. Moreover, the recent decline in personal savings rates is especially awkward for Keynesians who have generally viewed higher real personal income levels as conducive to *higher* savings rates rather than the lower ones that have actually ensued.

---

[1] I have used the 1989 figure to update the original 1984 article.

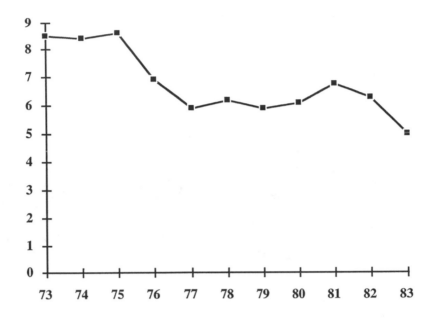

Source: U.S. Department of Commerce

Figure 27.1. Personal saving as percent of personal disposable income.

Nor does supply-side economics solve the puzzle. Reducing taxes on income and capital gains, and providing increased tax shelters for retirement accounts, were supposed by supply-siders to strengthen incentives to save. Yet the Reagan Administration has provided these inducements and, mirabile dictu, personal savings rates have declined!

Perhaps the passage of time is part of the explanation: The tax changes may have to be in effect for a longer period if people are to adjust their behavior accordingly. Moreover, the structure of taxes, as well as their rates, still provides a disincentive to save. When interest income that's received from savings is subject to tax, while interest payments to meet borrowing costs are tax deductible, the result is an incentive to borrow and spend rather than to save and lend. (It's worth noting that in Japan, interest income on savings deposits is tax exempt.)

Inflationary expectations are yet another important, if elusive, factor affecting savings: If people expect prices to be higher in the future, they'll be disinclined to save. Although there was a dramatic abatement of inflation in the early 1980s, skepticism about its permanence has probably not yet been dispelled. Disbelief that price stability will be maintained perhaps accounts for a disposition to spend while prices are relatively attractive, rather than to save for a future when dollars may be worth substantially less.

Although the determinants of savings rates—why they rise and fall, and why they're much higher in some economies than in others— are at best imperfectly understood, the subject deserves more analysis, discussion, and debate than it has received. Instead of repeating the familiar and almost ritualized arguments about budget deficits and how they can be reduced, it would be a step forward if presidential and other candidates were to address the even more important issue of private savings and how they can be increased.

Postaudit

The low U.S. savings rate remained a serious problem throughout the 1980s. Personal savings fell further—to 3 and 4 percent in the second half of the decade. By 1989, the personal rate had risen somewhat (to about 5 percent of disposable income). The outlook for gross savings is brighter in the 1990s because of prospective increases in Social Security surpluses and decreases in defense spending, among other reasons.

28

What Comes After
Gramm-Rudman-Hollings?

It is not too early to consider what, if any, changes in U.S. federal budget processes should follow Gramm-Rudman-Hollings (GRH).

Besides GRH, the principal proposals in contention for revamping the process are a balanced-budget amendment to the constitution, and a presidential line-item veto.

From the standpoint of sustaining long-term economic growth, none of these measures would be as meritorious as another: namely, requiring that the rate of growth in total federal spending should be no greater than the rate of GNP growth. This rule would prevent the ratio between government spending and GNP from rising in the future as it characteristically has in the past.

Two central facts provide support for establishing such a cap on spending growth. First, there is a generally significant negative relationship between the rate of economic growth and the size of the government sector (as measured by government spending as a ratio to GNP, or by the tax take as a ratio to GNP). Depending on which measure of government size is used, as well as a number of other factors (for example, the particular countries and the time period considered), research done both at RAND and the World Bank suggests that for each increase of 1 percent in the size of government, long-term economic growth decreases between 0.1 percent and 0.6 percent annually in both developed and developing countries.

Second, while the peacetime growth of federal government spending has been perennial and seemingly inexorable (even under

---

A slightly abbreviated version of this essay was published under the title "After Gramm-Rudman, Look to Spending Cap" by the Wall Street Journal *on June 26, 1986.*

the Reagan Administration this ratio rose from 21 to 24 percent),[1] the real increase in federal spending in any particular year has tended to be smaller when the federal budget deficit was larger in the *preceding* year. Between 1963 and 1984, a 1 percent rise in the real budget deficit in any particular year lowered the next year's increase in real outlays (after subtracting interest payments on the federal debt) by approximately $3.1 billion below what would have been expected absent the previous year's deficit. Evidently, larger deficits do have some restraining effect on congressional proclivities to spend.

That real budget outlays continued to rise along with rising deficits is not inconsistent with this finding; increases in government spending would have been still larger if the deficits had been smaller.

These relationships suggest the inherent shortcomings of the proposed balanced-budget amendment or of any successor to GRH: These proposals would not prevent increases in government spending above the rate of increase in GNP, if the then-president were less adamantly opposed to tax increases than Ronald Reagan. Consequently, under a budget-balancing proposal unrelated to a cap on spending growth, a strong possibility exists that the ratio of government spending to GNP would continue to rise, thereby resulting in downward pressure on economic growth.

The budget-balancing resolution, which has in the past been rejected by the Senate, would have capped spending growth by linking the requirement for an annually balanced federal budget to a restriction on the rate of growth in tax revenues. However, this restriction is omitted from the budget-balancing resolution that thirty-two state legislatures have already approved, as the basis for a constitutional convention.

One advantage of a presidential line-item veto is that it would not inherently lose the restraining effects of deficits on the growth of government spending. However, the veto power would still leave open the possibility of disproportionately large increases in government spending if a subsequent president's use of it were not especially focused on reducing spending.

---

[1] If spending by state and local government is included, the total government spending ratio for the United States is currently about 35 percent. Among the Western European countries, the comparable ratio is about 46 percent, while that for Japan is about 20 percent.

Numerous objections to the ratio cap on the growth of government spending can be cited. For example, the ratio cap would make the fiscal system inflexible and unable to respond to emergencies such as acute domestic recession or national security threats. Furthermore, such a cap might simply lead to a relative increase in spending by state and local governments, with similarly perverse effects on long-term aggregate economic growth. Finally, our ability to forecast prospective rates of growth in real GNP is so limited that implementation of the proposed proportional cap on spending growth would be infeasible.

These objections can be readily answered. In the event of overriding national needs for larger government outlays, Congress could suspend the cap, thereby allowing the growth rate of spending to exceed the growth rate of GNP for perhaps a year at a time. That this could be done expeditiously in the event of a national security or other emergency does not imply that it should be made easy; for example, a supermajority of the Congress might be required to temporarily suspend the cap. Public attention would then be activated by the suspension, thereby tending to limit the likelihood that it would be done casually. If in the absence of formal suspension, congressional appropriations nevertheless exceeded the cap, the president could be authorized to apply across-the-board cuts to reduce appropriations or to sequester them to keep spending below the cap.

With respect to possible expansion of spending by state and local governments as a result of the cap on federal spending, two counter-arguments can be given: first, some devolution along these lines is probably desirable and in keeping with the so-called "new federalism" advocated by every administration from President Kennedy's to President Reagan's; and second, nearly all of the state constitutions require a balanced budget, thereby constraining state governments' spending levels. The California constitution already places a cap on the growth of state and local government spending by limiting it to changes in population and inflation. (In contrast to conventional views about California's relaxed life-style, that state's budget process is considerably more disciplined and rigorous than most, and certainly more so than that of the federal government.)

Finally, while it is true that the forecasting problem makes the proportional cap on spending growth difficult to implement in any particular year, this is equally true of the budget balancing amendment, and of GRH. Both would require the forecasting of revenues, and these in turn are sensitive to forecasts of GNP. Moreover, mistaken decisions due to forecasting errors would not be disabling for the proportional spending cap; mistakes in one year could be redressed in the next.

In sum, unlike other proposals for controlling government spending, limiting the rate of growth in spending to the growth of GNP has the advantage of flexibility (for example, it would still allow deficits to be considered as an appropriate instrument of fiscal policy in special circumstances), as well as the distinct advantage of focusing on the main issue, namely the ratio of government spending to GNP, rather than on the secondary, if not unimportant, issue of achieving a fiscal balance. Focusing on the main issue would also promote increased effectiveness of government spending by obliging Congress and the administration to concentrate on the allocation of a constrained budget rather than on how much is to be spent.

Postaudit

Restricting growth of government spending to no more than the GNP growth rate still seems eminently sensible!

29

What's Wrong with "Trickle-Down"?

What's wrong with "trickle-down"?

From the clamor over David Stockman's trickle-down gaffe, one would infer that the obvious answer is: Everything!

As a means of improving the economy's performance, trickle-down is unfair, ineffective, and ill-conceived. It smacks of special privilege and special interests, making the rich richer while hinting that the rest of us may benefit later on. It is elitist, undemocratic, and perhaps even un-American!

But, wait a minute. Rhetoric aside, the question can't be seriously answered without two prior steps: defining what trickle-down actually means and considering the alternatives.

Asked about his use of the term as quoted in William Greider's *Atlantic* article, Stockman admitted he really wasn't "certain what 'trickle-down' means." You will look in vain for it in economics texts: Trickle-down is not part of the economist's formal code.

However, there are several plausible ways of describing it. One formulation is as follows. Measures to stimulate investment (by tax write-offs, accelerated depreciation, lower taxes on investment income, and so forth) will, in turn and in time, increase production and consumption throughout the economy. Since the investment share of gross national product is quite small (5 to 10 percent is a generous estimate), such measures really amount to providing incentives for the few, who do most of the investing, to generate subsequent benefits for the many: hence "trickle-down."

Ironically, this formulation is no less consistent with Keynesian demand-management economics than with Kemp-Roth supply-side economics. What it amounts to is the Keynesian investment multi-

---

A slightly abbreviated version of this essay was published under the title "The Case for 'Trickle-Down'" by the Los Angeles Times *on January 20, 1982.*

plier without some of the latter's technical trimmings: If an initial increase in investment can be stimulated, it will increase total output by an amount that eventually will exceed the initial increase in investment.

An example of this version of trickle-down, referred to by Stockman in his indiscreetly candid remarks, is the 1981 Economic Recovery Tax Act's reduction of the maximum tax rate on investment income from 70 to 50 percent.   Its intended supply-side effect is to strengthen incentives to save and invest, with the prospect of generating larger increases in output downstream, and thereby moving the economy forward.

Another version of trickle-down focuses not on numerical multipliers but on a vision of the capitalist system and what makes it work. The intellectual heritage in this case is Schumpeter and his theory of capitalism, rather than Keynes or supply-side economics.   This version emphasizes entrepreneurship and innovation as the mainsprings of economic growth and technological progress.

But the successful entrepreneurs and innovators are very few.   A larger number will try.   They will spot an opportunity for a new product, or a new way of producing an old one, and take the chance.   But only a few will achieve big successes.   Their imitators are more numerous, and their ultimate beneficiaries are the rest of us.   Providing an environment in which innovation and entrepreneurship can flourish is one way of trying to move a stagnant economy toward progress and growth. But the catalytic role of the few successful entrepreneurs is crucial.

Again, trickle-down.

So much for describing it.   What about the alternatives?

One set of alternatives seeks to bring about growth and progress by efforts from below, from the grass roots: not trickle-down but "bubble-up," so to speak—another term that is not in the economist's code.

West Germany's "codetermination" (mit Bestimmung) movement is an example.   Companies employing more than 1,000 workers are required to reserve half the seats on their corporate boards of directors for workers' representatives, who thereby participate directly in shaping corporate investment, employment, and production policies.

Yugoslavia's workers' councils, and Solidarity's proposed system of worker self-management in Poland, are other examples of efforts to promote change and progress from below rather than above.

An extreme version of bubble-up was Mao Tse Tung's cultural revolution in the 1960s, with its Luddite attacks on large scale production facilities and centralized decisionmaking, and its hapless experiment with small-scale technology and decentralized decision-making (recall the fiasco of "backyard" steel furnaces).

Another alternative to trickle-down is the "big-push" by government: centralized planning and investment to direct the economy along certain lines determined by a national plan. Direct government action may be the chosen instrument, or indirect measures—for example, tariff protection, subsidized loans, or preferential tax treatment—may be used instead, for the same ends.

The Soviet-type, centrally planned command economy is one variant of this approach. Perspective planning in France is a more permissive variant; although under the Mitterand government pre-1985 and post-1988 commands sometimes increased while permissiveness decreased.

What, then, is wrong with trickle-down? The generally accepted answer is arguable. Once trickle-down is defined and compared with the alternatives, the balance of advantage is not clear. The original metaphor sounds much worse than it really is, while the alternatives are uncertain at best and unpromising at least. Trickle-down isn't all wrong or all bad, and the alternatives aren't all right or all good.

An assessment of trickle-down is like an assessment of the process of growing older: The phenomenon is not entirely appealing, but it doesn't look so bad when compared with the alternatives!

Postaudit

Stockman is virtually forgotten, as is the Atlantic *article. "Trickle-down" has a faintly nostalgic ring to it. However, in light of the collapse of Soviet-type command economies, the general argument advanced in the article is even more convincing now than when it was written. The alternatives to so-called trickle-down—that is, to incentives that stimulate investment and entrepreneurship—are generally not effective.*

30

Is the Economy Poised or Paralyzed?

Seldom have the models and forecasters been as close to agreement as in their predictions of a meager recovery in the U.S. economy in 1982 to 1983. Both supply-side and Keynesian models registered similar forecasts of scanty U.S. economic growth in 1983, ranging from the Council of Economic Advisors' estimate of 1.5 to 2 percent, to the 2 to 3 percent estimates of the CBO, DRI, Wharton, Chase, and assorted other models in this crowded field. A similar consensus applies to their forecasts of 1983 unemployment (above 10 percent) and budget deficits ($190 to $200 billion).

The modelers seemed likely to be right. But the probability was, I surmised at the time, only two or three to one, rather than ten to one. Put another way, there are a number of reasons why these predictions seemed possibly to be quite wrong.

One reason is simply that these large econometric models of the U.S. economy have so often been wrong in the past in their year-in-advance forecasts of the economy's performance. Consequently, a consensus of gloomy forecasts provides almost as much ground for optimism as pessimism.

There are other and stronger reasons why the economy may do much better than expected. The most important and usually over-looked reason concerns the effect of increased price stability on spending decisions by business and households—especially house-holds. Just as inflation tends to stimulate current spending because prices are expected to be higher in the future, so deflation leads to postponement of current spending because prices are expected to be *lower* in the future. When prices eventually stabilize, the postponed spending that has accumulated will reach the market.

A slightly abbreviated version of this essay was published under the title, "Hidden Potential for Economic Takeoff?" by the Los Angeles Times *on February 4, 1983.*

Actually, the extraordinary reversal of inflation that occurred in the American economy in the past two years has not produced real deflation (falling prices), but *dis*inflation—that is, a dramatic slowing of the previous inflation. But the effect has been similar to that of falling prices for two reasons: first, because some prices actually were falling (gasoline, foods, certain electronic goods, and appliances), thereby nurturing expectations that they would continue to do so and that others might follow suit; and second, because the unspent income could realize a return (for example, from money market funds, money market deposit accounts, fixed debt) that was considerably higher than the sharply decreased rate at which prices continued to rise. For both reasons, incentives to postpone spending grew stronger as disinflation proceeded.

But this process, and these incentives, seemed to be nearing their end. In 1982, consumer prices rose only 3.9 percent (compared with 8.9 and 11.4 percent in 1981 and 1980, respectively), and in the last quarter of 1982 the increase was only three-tenths of 1 percent! This rate seemed unlikely to get lower. Indeed, some modest increase seemed more likely than a further decline. This, together with the declining yield on savings and the reduced cost of borrowing, meant that incentives would favor spending rather than postponing.

Moreover, the liquid assets available to finance this deferred spending were enormous. For example, between the first quarter of 1980 and the third quarter of 1982, household financial assets grew by over 30 percent, from $3.9 to $5.1 trillion. And continuation of foreign capital inflow seemed likely to add further to these already abundant means to finance increased spending.

If, and as, spending—especially household spending—rises, industry should be in a position to respond rapidly and efficiently. Starting from the 1982 low level of capacity utilization in manufacturing industry (then at only 68 percent compared with 79 percent in 1981), output could readily be increased without encountering bottlenecks of equipment, materials, or labor that otherwise would push prices upwards. Moreover, the weeding out of higher-cost firms through the painful spate of bankruptcies in the past year—the so-called "molting" of American industry—would be likely to enhance the efficiency with which production can respond to increased spending.

What is the bottom line? Unfortunately, it's blurred. All of the factors I've described could well make the economy more buoyant, and its prospects much brighter than suggested by the accepted forecasts. The economy may be poised for a rapid rate of annual growth of 5 or 6 percent rather than 2 percent, as well as for sharper reductions of unemployment and deficits, than those that were predicted.

On the other hand, all of these factors might not be enough. High rates of current unemployment may tend to discourage spending by those who remain employed, as a precaution in case their own jobs are lost. Pressure on money markets from government borrowing may sustain excessively high real interest rates that will depress business investment. And reduced access to foreign markets, due to both recession and protection, may diminish exports.

The bottom line is admittedly blurred. Yet the likelihood of substantial economic improvement is much greater than suggested by the melancholy consensus of the models and modelers.

Postaudit

As it turned out, 1983 was a year of extraordinarily rapid growth that reached the higher levels suggested as a possibility when this was published in February 1983. The article also conveys at least a hint of what has turned out to be the longest (approaching eight years) sustained expansion in the peacetime economic history of the 20th century!

31

Reaganomics, Keynesian Economics, and the Current Recovery

However perverse and "unfair" the record of Reaganomics seemed to its opponents during the first two years of the Reagan Administration, they must concede that its status and prospects became enormously better in its third year.

Consider the following indicators. In the first half of 1983, GNP grew at an annual rate of over 5.6 percent net of inflation, compared with prior forecasts of only 3 to 4 percent. Consumer prices have increased only 2 percent, about as close to price stability as our inflation-prone and indexed economy is likely to achieve. Employment increased by nearly 500,000 in the first half of the year, and another 500,000 in July; unemployment, though still high at 9.5 percent, fell by nearly 1 percent. Manufacturing capacity utilization increased from 68 to 75 percent; and labor productivity rose, while labor costs per unit of output actually decreased for the first time in eight years.

How can these improvements be explained? A strong resurgence of consumer demand is the principal explanation. In the first half of 1983, total consumer spending increased over 10 percent, thereby providing a powerful demand stimulus to the entire economy, which is reflected in the previously cited indicators.

It is both odd and ironic that Reaganomics is undergoing redemption at the hands of consumer demand: "odd" because unexpected, and "ironic" because, hitherto, consumer demand has occupied a much more central role in the liberal Democratic policies of Keynesian economics than the conservative Republican policies of Reaganomics.

A slightly abbreviated version of this essay was published under the title "Hold the Cheers for Reaganomics" by the Los Angeles Times *on August 18, 1983.*

In Keynesian economics, boosting consumer demand is essential for economic recovery because output and employment are assumed to be highly responsive to demand. Hence, Keynesian economics is often designated as "demand management" or "demand-side" economics.

By contrast, the principal components of "classical" Reaganomics—reduced taxes (especially business taxes), diminished government regulation, and reduced government spending—are only peripherally concerned with consumer spending. Instead, Reaganomics focuses on the need to lower costs and increase incentives on the supply side of the economy. (Even reductions in personal income taxes have received their main justification in Reaganomic policies as a means of inducing supply-side responses: namely, increased labor effort, higher productivity, and increased consumer *saving*, rather than spending.) Hence, the familiar "supply-side" label that has appropriately been applied to Reaganomics.

In Keynesian economics, demand occupies center stage, and supply is an understudy. In Reaganomics, the roles are exactly reversed. How then can Reaganomics claim credit for an economic recovery triggered by economic actions and actors to which it accords only a secondary role?

The answer is that such claims warrant seasoning with the usual grains of salt. The recovery has occurred through a mechanism that was neither articulated nor anticipated by the original proponents of Reaganomics. That mechanism is the termination of rapid inflation in 1981, its replacement by disinflation (a dramatic slowing of the previous inflation) in mid-1982, the achievement of price stability—at least temporarily—in late 1982, and the ensuing jump in consumer demand in 1983. In turn, the suppression and extrusion of inflation in 1981 and 1982 are attributable to the admittedly painful monetary restraint of Federal Reserve policy rather than to the supply-side policies directly advocated by the White House.

When inflation gallops, as it did in the high double-digit years of 1979 and 1980, consumer spending is stimulated by expectations that future prices will exceed current ones. Eventually, this stimulus may be capped by a fear that something must be saved against the day when the bubble will burst. In any event, if and when inflation slows down (disinflation) as it did in 1981, and some prices actually fall as they did in 1982, consumer spending contracts for two reasons: first, because consumers expect future prices to be *less* than current ones, so it makes sense to defer spending; and second, because consumers feel insecure about their own continued employment, so precautionary saving increases.

During 1982, consumers retreated from the market, in the process amassing a huge volume of liquid assets: Household financial assets grew by 16 percent between 1981 and the end of 1982, from $4,657 billion to $5,395 billion. Reversal of this retreat and the resurgence of consumer spending was triggered by price stability, further galvanized by a suspicion that stability may be only temporary. With stable prices, there is no longer a reason to defer spending in anticipation of lower prices in the future; with the suspicion that stability may be temporary, there is every reason to reenter the market quickly before prices start to rise again.

In sum, disinflation and price stability account for the resurgence of consumer spending, and output and employment have responded to this rise in demand in nice conformity to the precepts of Keynesian economics. The result has been the substantial recovery that has occurred thus far in 1983. None of this is really due to Reaganomics, whose supply-side effects remain to be realized. Indeed, the likelihood that these effects will ensue henceforth—albeit after a considerably longer lag than their advocates had originally envisaged—provides a strong reason for believing the economic recovery will be sustained for a considerably longer time than the often erring, but always undaunted, forecasters have recently predicted.

Although Reaganomics may claim some credit for the favorable turn of economic events, the claim should be somewhat muted. The boost to consumer demand, and thereby to the entire economy, resulted not from Reaganomics but from the price stability induced by the Federal Reserve's monetary restraint, with only moral rather than operational support from the administration. Ironically, Keynesian economics provides a better guide to understanding and explaining the recovery than does Reaganomics.

Postaudit

In longer-run terms than those reflected in the article, supply-side economics (Reaganomics) and demand-side economics (Keynesianism) are opposite sides of the same coin: The former emphasizes incentives to motivate producers, while the latter focuses on the stimulus provided by and to consumers.

32

A Panglossian View of the Economy

There are ample grounds for greater optimism about the economy's prospects than the gloomy consensus that often prevails.

This consensus is reflected in the foreboding phrases recently emanating from most of the frequently cited commentators. For example, "an economy that has made little progress" (Data Resources); "a stalled economy" (Economic Policy Institute); "the trade deficit is an economic disaster" (National Association of Manufacturers); "warning signals flashing 'trouble ahead'" (*New York Times* op-ed); "no revival in sight for the industrial side of the economy" (Shearson Lehman Brothers); "the inevitable impact of those untamed killer deficits" (*Newsweek*); and "continued, sizable deterioration of the trade balance [and] a further drag on GNP" (Institute for International Economics).

The prevailing consensus is not only gloomy, it is also procrustean: Indicators that appear inconsistent with it are reinterpreted to prevent even the slightest ray of light from obscuring the prevailing gloom. Thus, when the index of leading indicators rises, it is dismissed as due to "robust financial markets, not to underlying economic strength" (Shearson Lehman Brothers), as though the two were quite unrelated.

There are several reasons for skepticism about this portentous view. One reason is that the forecasters have erred so often in the past that there is little ground for expecting them to be accurate now. While this provides some grounds for confidence that they'll be wrong again, fortunately there are other, more substantial reasons for at least moderate optimism now. Our current economic problems (was there ever a period when the U.S. economy was completely

A slightly abbreviated version of this essay was published under the title, "A Silver Lining in the Economy" in the New York Times *on September 11, 1985.*

problem-free?) have been either overstated, or are associated with readily accessible remedies.

Consider, for example, the three most evidently serious problems: the two deficits—budget and trade—and international debt.

The federal budget deficit was forecast to be about $200 billion for 1986 and thereafter. Surely, this imbalance is undesirable. However, it is equally sure that it is not disabling. From the standpoint of the effect of government borrowing on credit markets, the federal deficit should first of all be viewed in conjunction with the forecast budget *surpluses* of the states. This shrinks the consolidated federal and state deficit for 1986 to about $170 or $180 billion. If the Senate and House can sustain, in the appropriations process, the modest spending reductions they agreed to in setting their budget ceilings, the consolidated deficit figure will decline by another $40 or $50 billion. The consolidated 1986 deficit then shrinks to between 3 and 3.5 percent of the GNP.

Although this is still large, in relative terms it is well below deficit ratios that Japan has regularly exceeded while sustaining its high rates of economic growth during the past ten years. Actually, the comparative international growth experience of other countries as well as Japan suggests a different, and neglected, lesson: Sustained economic growth can more easily be reconciled with deficits of this size than with total government *spending* at our current scale—over 36 percent of the GNP.

In short, government allocation of such large shares of total resources—including redistributive allocations that may impinge on incentives—constitutes a more serious constraint on long-term growth than the consolidated budget deficit. For example, if the deficits were reduced (say, by tax increases), while governmental resource allocations are not, the economy's prospects would be drearier than if government spending were reduced while the deficit is not (due, say, to tax decreases).

Next, consider the "other" deficit. The 1984 trade deficit was $123 billion, and that forecast for 1985 was $140 billion. Only an antiquated yet persistent neomercantilism explains use of the exaggerated term "disaster" to characterize what is bound to be only a transitory problem. The trade deficit is attributable to the fact that U.S. investment exceeds domestic savings. The deficit thus facilitates a higher level of U.S. investment—hence, future U.S. growth and higher productivity—than would be feasible if the trade account were in balance or in surplus at the present level of U.S. savings. That the trade deficit has been accompanied by a high rather than declining exchange value of the dollar as would normally be expected, indicates simply that holders of nondollar assets have been more bullish in their evaluation of the U.S. economy than of the foreign economies in which their nondollar assets were previously held. This accounts for their wish to hold increasing amounts of dollar assets, thereby increasing the demand for dollar assets and bidding up the dollar's exchange value, until quite recently.

Moreover, there is an automatic mechanism that assures that the trade deficit will be transitory. If and when U.S. investment declines, or U.S. savings rise, or assetholders change their evident if recently somewhat diminished preference for dollar assets, the trade deficit will be reduced and eventually eliminated. While any or several of these changes could occur abruptly and disruptively, there are stronger reasons for expecting the adjustment to come about gradually and smoothly. The decline in the dollar's value after March 1985 suggests that a gradual adjustment process has already begun.

Finally, the international debt problem is also subject to more benign, as well as more accurate, interpretations than those reflected by the hand-wringers' prevailing consensus.

For example, it is seldom recognized that the real costs, as distinct from the accounting costs, of the $500 billion of international debt owed by the developing countries, as well as by Eastern Europe and the Soviet Union, *have already been incurred*. The real costs are the goods and services, the commodities and machinery, previously exported to the debtor countries by the creditors. These costs represent the benefits forgone by the creditors (principally but not exclusively by the United States), because their factors of production—labor, capital, and materials—were used for the benefit of external borrowers rather than for internal investment, research and development, and consumption in the lending countries themselves. Consider, for example, how much higher U.S. productivity would be if a significant share of the loans made in the 1970s to Latin America had instead financed new investment and research and development in the United States, or if Western European loans to the Soviet Union and Eastern Europe had instead financed investment and R&D within the European Economic Community.

The accounting problem arises from the fact that these debts are subject to widely differing repayment prospects, as suggested by discounts of from 10 to 90 percent currently prevailing on the secondary debt market for these assets. If and as the commercial banks holding these assets are obliged to revalue their balance sheets accordingly, bank losses will ensue. However, so long as the net capital, or shareholders' equity, of these banks remains even slightly positive—which can and ultimately would be assured by the Federal Reserve Bank, as lender of last resort—this adjustment will simply mean a reduction (in some cases, a very substantial reduction) in the market values of bank stocks. Shareholders of the major bank holding companies would thus lose, although depositors would not. But even if the share prices of Citicorp, Manufacturers Hanover, or Chase were to fall to single digit values, there need be no great stress for the economy as whole. Indeed, that's the way markets work: The stockholders of these banks have experienced large profits and dividends in the past (their stocks have outperformed the market as a whole during the past ten years); it is not unreasonable or inappropriate that they may experience substantial losses in the future.

In short, even if the economic outlook falls somewhat short of the Panglossian "best of all possible worlds," it is much brighter than the picture portrayed by the gloomy consensus.

Postaudit

It should be evident from this piece, as well as earlier and later ones during the 1980s, that my view of the economy's performance and prospects was persistently more optimistic than that of the consensus among most academic economists and most business forecasters. With the clarity of hindsight, and in light of 91 months of sustained economic growth (as of June 1990), it's also evident that this more optimistic view was more accurate than the consensus one.

33

The Muddle over High Interest
Rates and the Overvalued Dollar

According to an argument prematurely accepted as valid in much of Western Europe, as well as in various political, financial, and media circles in the United States, high U.S. interest rates and the overvalued dollar, which they ostensibly cause, are preventing economic recovery in Europe and threatening to abort it in the United States. The near unanimity with which certain influential commentators on both sides of the Atlantic have adopted this position should alert us to the possibility that it may be flawed. Well, it is!

The argument involves several parts. First, it is said, high U.S. interest rates draw capital from Europe and elsewhere into the United States. (The high rates themselves are usually attributed to large U.S. budgetary deficits, although there is some disagreement on this point. Other explanations include the overly tight—or alternatively, fitfully loose—monetary policy of Mr. Volcker, and the distorting effects of a U.S. tax structure that converts nominal interest rates of 12 or 13 percent into after-tax, inflation-adjusted rates of only 3 or 4 percent.)

Second, it is argued, the attraction of foreign capital to the United States depletes the supply of savings and financing available for European investment. The resulting upward pressure on European interest rates suppresses nascent recovery there before it can gather momentum.

Third, the inflow of foreign capital to the United States allegedly boosts the exchange value of the dollar above what is warranted by the dollar's purchasing power. The result, so the argument goes, is that U.S. exports are less able to compete in foreign markets, and foreign imports acquire a competitive advantage in the U.S. market.

A slightly abbreviated version of this essay was published under the title "The Muscular Dollar" by the New York Times *on November 8, 1983.*

For both reasons, unemployment in the United States stays high and may rise again, and recovery here will be set back.

So goes the argument. What about its flaws?

One flaw lies in ascribing to high U.S. interest rates the exclusive, or at least predominant, responsibility for the dollar's high exchange value, rather than recognizing that they are only one among several causes, and probably not the most important one. The second flaw is failing to recognize that a strong dollar has multiple effects, some of which stimulate recovery abroad even while others may damp it at home.

In a generally free foreign exchange market, such as we currently have, exchange parities depend on the relative demands for and supplies of the various currencies. That the dollar has appreciated in the past 18 months relative to the principal European currencies by 16 to 40 percent (the lower figure relates to the German mark, the upper one to the French franc, while the pound and lira are in between), simply means that the demand for dollars by holders of foreign currencies has increased relative to the available dollar supply. Just as the price of a vintage wine rises if consumer demand for it increases, so the "price" of dollars will rise if demand for dollars increases among holders of foreign currencies.

What accounts for this increased demand for dollars? There are many contributing causes. First, foreign demand for dollars has risen because foreign assetholders want to buy U.S. equities in the belief that stock prices will increase as progress of the American recovery brings with it higher sales and profits for U.S. businesses. The sharp rise of over 55 percent in the past year in the New York Stock Exchange index has amply justified this belief.

Second, demand for dollars has risen because of the desire by foreign assetholders to buy real property in the United States. Notwithstanding the appreciated dollar, real estate prices in the United States—even in such premium markets as New York, Los Angeles, and their environs—are still lower than in London, Paris and Tokyo.

Third, demand for dollars has increased because holders of foreign assets believe—justifiably, it would seem—that control of inflation in the United States is, and is likely to remain, more effective than abroad. Acquiring dollar assets provides protection against this financial risk.

Finally, dollar demand has strengthened because of the relative immunity from political risk enjoyed by dollar assets compared with non-dollar assets. Nationalization of businesses and banks by a Socialist government in France, electoral gains in the West German Bundestag by the frenetic "Greens," and the choice by the British Labour Party of a leader who is apparently anti-NATO, anti-defense, and anti-United States, makes holders of assets in those countries understandably anxious to relinquish the assets they have in exchange for the dollars they covet.

Estimating how much weight should be assigned to each of the five sources (the four above plus high interest rates) in explaining the dollar's appreciation has not been attempted, and would be extremely difficult. Assigning equal weight to the five is no less foolish, though perhaps less disingenuous, than assigning all of the weight to high interest rates alone. Between 1980 and 1982, officially reported foreign holdings of dollar assets in the United States increased by 60 percent, from $54.9 to $87.9 billion. No doubt all five reasons for the dollar's appreciation have influenced these acquisitions.

Simply put, the dollar's exchange value has risen relative to other currencies because it has become more valuable in terms of the various "values" or aims that assetholders seek. So, the first flaw in the original argument amounts to a truism: The dollar's value has increased because it has become more valuable to people who formerly held nondollar assets. The dollar is no more "overvalued" now because it exchanges for 8 French francs than it was 18 months ago when it exchanged for 5.75.

The second flaw derives from the fact that a strong dollar has positive, growth-promoting effects, as well as negative, growth-restraining ones. From the standpoint of Western Europe, the stronger dollar represents capital outflow, hence a reduction of funds for domestic investment and upward pressure on European interest rates. Yet at the same time the strong dollar also improves the competitive position of European exports compared with U.S. exports, both in world markets and in the American market, thereby boosting European employment and production and strengthening incentives for European investment.

From the U.S. standpoint, the strong dollar impairs the competitive position of U.S. exporters, as well as intensifying import competition in the U.S. market. Yet at the same time the strong dollar also improves prospects for servicing the enormous international dollar debt of the precariously situated Third World debtors (Brazil, Mexico, and Argentina), the more robust but still acutely export-dependent ones (Korea and Taiwan), and at least one major debtor among the developed countries (France).   Inasmuch as the international debt predicament is itself a serious threat to economic recovery, and to the solvency of the principal American banks, the stimulus to dollar-earning exports that is provided by a strong dollar is a boon, rather than a bane to the U.S. recovery itself.

In sum, the "high-interest-rate-strong-dollar" chorus should change its plaintive tune.   The strength of the dollar isn't primarily due to high interest rates, and a strong dollar has as much good as bad to be said for it.

Postaudit

In the seven intervening years since this was written, the dollar continued to climb through 1985, thereafter weakened substantially through mid-1989 (by nearly 50 percent in terms of yen), thereafter rising through mid-1990 (by about 30 percent).   Throughout this period, the multiple factors and explanations cited in the article continued to operate, while varying in their relative influence, more or less in general accord with the discussion presented in 1983.

34

Those Puzzling Interest Rates

Why are interest rates so high? The question has often dominated economic discussion, resulting in a remarkable consensus: Everyone agrees that no one knows the answer!

On theoretical grounds, interest rates "should" (and normally do) equal the expected rate of inflation plus the real rate of return on capital. But current figures are way out of line. Inflation, as an indicator of "expected" inflation, is now running below 8 percent. And historically the return on capital runs about 3 or 4 percent. Add them together and interest rates "should" be 11 to 12 percent. But prevailing rates are now about 16 percent.

That leaves a lot to be explained—4 to 5 percent, or between one quarter and one third of the current interest rate. So what explains the excessive cost of borrowing money these days?

It seems clear that there isn't a single explanation for high interest rates, but many contributory ones: inflationary expectations; the large government deficits, and government borrowing to finance them; and uncertainties about Federal Reserve policies, including both worries that these policies will remain restrictive and fears that they won't.

While all of these play a part, another important explanation is generally overlooked: the tax deductibility of interest payments. Its special importance can be grasped by slightly reformulating the original question. The result will suggest both an answer to the question, and a way of reducing pressure on credit markets, thereby easing interest rates.

Interest rates—the price of credit—are determined by the interaction between lenders and borrowers, just as commodity prices are determined by the interaction between sellers and buyers. That lenders

A slightly abbreviated version of this essay was published under the title "Take the Tax Deduction Out of Borrowing and Interest Rates Will Fall" by the Los Angeles Times *on June 27, 1982.*

are willing to lend at prevailing high rates is not puzzling; the reason is quite simply that "the price is right." The problem lies in explaining the behavior of borrowers.

Therefore, rather than asking, "Why are interest rates so high?" ask instead, "Why are borrowers willing to pay such high rates?" Or alternatively, "How can they afford to do so?"

Of course, borrowers come in many shapes and sizes, but they can generally be divided into three categories: government, business, and households.

Among the three categories, the government's willingness and ability to pay high interest rates is easiest to explain: Once spending and tax legislation have been enacted, the amount of government borrowing is mandated by law. Government will borrow this amount, regardless of the rate it has to pay.

For business to be willing to borrow, its expected real rate of return on borrowed money must at least equal the difference between the cost of borrowing and the rate of inflation. For example, if interest rates are 16 percent and inflation is 7 or 8 percent, the real rate of return expected by businesses must be at least 8 or 9 percent. Otherwise, borrowing will simply add more to costs than revenues, thereby reducing earnings.

Under current economic conditions, few businesses can meet this condition.

For households, the situation is different. Households borrow largely for consumption, not for investment. Most household borrowing is devoted to purchases of durable consumers' goods—cars, appliances, recreational gear, and housing. These purchases yield services over a long period, but they are consumption, not production, services. For households to be willing to borrow, the benefits of doing so must exceed the costs. Inflation automatically provides some benefit because borrowing makes it possible for households to buy at currently lower prices rather than the higher ones expected to prevail later.

Further benefits from borrowing arise from what economists call "pure time preference" (or just plain "eagerness"): Even with stable prices, earlier consumption is generally preferred to later, and borrowing permits earlier consumption.

The household's cost of borrowing has a special twist to it because interest payments can be deducted from taxable income. Hence, the household's cost of borrowing is not the market rate of interest, but rather that rate adjusted for the deductibility of interest payments from taxable income.

If, for example, a particular household's income is subject to a marginal tax rate (federal plus state) of 40 percent, and the prevailing rate of interest is 16 percent, the household's net cost of borrowing works out to only 9.6 percent (40 percent of the interest payments would otherwise have been drained away as taxes, so this interest expense really costs the household nothing). Tax deductibility of interest payments thus makes the household's net cost of borrowing much less than the market interest rate.

So, if the rate of inflation is 8 percent, and the household is willing to pay a premium as low as 1.7 percent to be able to consume sooner (by borrowing), it will go ahead and borrow when interest rates are 16 percent because the benefit from borrowing (8 percent plus 1.7 percent) exceeds its effective cost (9.6 percent). Of course, for households with higher incomes and higher marginal tax rates, the net costs of borrowing are lower still.

The answer to the earlier question is now clear: Among borrowers willing to pay the prevailing high interest rates, consumer borrowers are prominent because they are able to avoid a substantial fraction of the nominal interest charge. Quantitatively, consumers loom large in the credit market: Total consumer borrowing, including residential mortgage borrowing, in 1981 was over $500 billion, more than three times greater than borrowing by nonfarm business. While most new consumer borrowing replaces prior consumer debt that is repaid, a shrinking of total "float" would appreciably ease the pressure of credit demand on aggregate credit supply.

This account also suggests how interest rates might be lowered: by capping the tax deductibility of household interest payments. The result would likely be a considerable reduction in credit demands by consumers, and lower interest rates.

Moreover, since higher-income groups derive relatively greater benefits from the tax deductibility of interest payments, reducing the deductibility allowance by, say, one third or one half, would impinge more on these groups. In the semantics of public finance, this would therefore be a "progressive" change in the tax structure.

Finally, putting such a cap on the interest rate deduction would tend to make borrowing relatively easier for business than for consumers, thereby facilitating the transfer of aggregate savings toward investment in plant and equipment and away from durable consumer goods and housing. Such a transfer would contribute to a more productive and healthy economy in the long run.

Postaudit

The numbers and arithmetic have, not surprisingly, changed since 1982, but the argument and its conclusions remain valid. Mid-1990 borrowing rates are about 11 percent (versus 16 percent in 1982). Inflation is about 4.5 percent (versus 8 percent then). With a marginal tax rate of 28 percent, the net cost of consumer borrowing works out to 3.5 percent, about twice that of 1982. Disincentives for adding to consumer debt have thus been strengthened. By lowering corporate tax rates, as well as personal income tax rates, the tax reform of 1986 increased after-tax incentives for business borrowing while decreasing those for consumer borrowing.

Nevertheless, further tightening of the deductibility of household interest payments, as proposed in the article, is still desirable. One way of implementing this, in a "revenue neutral" way, would be to combine a proportionate cap on the deductibility of interest payments (say, 50 percent) with an equivalent deductibility allowance of interest earnings. Japan's tax structure contains provisions of this sort, thereby contributing to higher savings and lower interest rates.

35

Stocks, Brokers, and Computers

One of the distinctive characteristics of the stock market is that the middleman benefits, at least in the short run, from price volatility. The benefits arise because the volume of market transactions tends to be higher when prices are either rising or falling than when they are stable, and the yield from commissions depends on the volume of transactions.

Of course, if prices are "too" volatile over "too" long a period, these benefits may well be offset or exceeded by a countervailing loss: The market may contract because investors liquidate their holdings and move their assets elsewhere. But whether this countervailing effect will be sufficient in the long run to offset the incentives that are created for volatility in the short run is unclear. To put the point another way, in some circumstances the contracting effects to be expected from market volatility in the long run may be an insufficient deterrent to uncoordinated, but immensely profitable, actions by brokers that promote volatility in the short run.

One need not, and should not, impugn either the motives of brokers or their genuine concern for the interests of their clients to suggest that the prevalent incentives may induce brokers to be especially receptive to indications of *either* a prospective rise or a prospective fall in the market, and to advise their clients accordingly (these incentives are reduced, but not eliminated, by competition in brokerage fees and by institutional trading).

To be sure, where market indicators, or the underlying "fundamentals," are ambiguous (as they quite frequently are), brokers will tend to favor signs that point to a prospective market rise over signs of a prospective fall, because commissions in the former in-

A slightly abbreviated version of this essay was published under the title "Trading in Your Broker for a Machine" in the Los Angeles Times *on December 27, 1987.*

stance benefit from higher prices as well as a larger transactions volume.   However, a prospective fall in prices may generally be preferred, from the standpoint of brokers, to a stable market.   Hence, if the credibility of a further rise in market prices begins to wane (due, for example, to unprecedentedly high price/earnings ratios), as was surely the case following the extraordinary bull market of the months before October 19, 1987, brokers will collectively although uncoordinatedly fix on the down-trending scenario as an appealing one in terms both of credibility and self-interest.

Something of this sort was probably operative just prior to "Black Monday." Although market values declined by 25 percent, the resulting anguish was probably somewhat relieved by the three- or fourfold jump in transactions volume and the commissions accompanying it.

This does not in any sense imply that the crash was engineered, nor does it gainsay that there were economic fundamentals underlying the crash (for example, the immediately preceding rise in interest rates and the prospect of further ones, a growing possibility of inflation, and the peaking of price earnings ratios for equities).   Instead, it simply suggests that some distinctive attributes of the stock market can contribute to an unusual degree of volatility.

At a time when computerized program trading is a currently favored bête noire in explaining the market's recent escapade, it may come as a surprise to suggest, as I will below, that another form of computerized trading might ease this problem. The idea is to apply in the securities industry an innovation in communications technology that has increasingly been adopted in the banking industry—the automated teller machine (ATM). Stock market investors could place orders to buy or sell stocks from what might be called "automated broker machines" (ABMs), which would be located, as are ATMs, at numerous convenient locations, including but not restricted to brokers' offices, and accessible to both the homes and working places of investors. Eventually, orders could even be made through a modem-linked PC in investors' homes.

ABM orders could be screened and validated through a computerized scanning of an individual investor's portfolio, cash holdings, allowable credit threshold, and the standard suitability rules, based on records maintained by the broker's central processing unit.

The ABM service could be paid for by a (monthly or yearly) common-carrier service charge based on the investor's house account, and analogous to the monthly charge for telephone service. Like the ATM service provided by banks, no additional charge would be levied for each individual order to purchase or sell stocks. Consequently, revenues from ABMs would not be affected by short-run changes in transactions volume.

Just as the "T" in ATM reduces the demand for bank tellers, so the "B" in ABM would reduce the demand for brokers, or at least for account executives. Instead, the demand for computer programmers might be increased, and account executives would become analysts, consultants, and advisers to a greater extent, since their roles as salespeople would diminish. In the process, the incentives created by brokerage commissions that thereby promote market volatility would be attenuated if not eliminated.

Postaudit

Notwithstanding the cutbacks in Wall Street houses since the 1987 market stumble, the middleman function inadvertently, unconsciously, and inevitably contributes to market volatility. The ABM proposal that I made in 1987 is still germane, probably less ahead of its time now than it was then.

International Dimensions

36

The Trade Deficit:
Myths and Realities

In popular discussion of economic matters, frequent repetition of erroneous or dubious propositions sometimes results in their public acceptance. Frequently, familiarity with the propositions, rather than their accuracy, accounts for the conventional wisdom.

Consider the following bits of conventional wisdom about the U.S. trade deficit:

- A trade surplus contributes to economic strength, while a trade deficit detracts from it.

- The U.S. trade deficit arises because U.S. exports are unable to compete in protected foreign markets.

- Some form of U.S. protectionism is desirable to protect and defend our economic recovery.

- The trade deficit signifies a loss of American jobs and increased unemployment.

Each of these commonly accepted beliefs is either wrong or at best only a small piece of a much larger, and sharply contrasting, truth. Accuracy would warrant correction or major reformulation of each proposition along the following lines.

First, exports actually subtract from a country's available resources, while imports add resources and thereby provide the means by which the importing economy can invest more and consume more

A slightly abbreviated version of this essay was published in the Los Angeles Times *on December 26, 1985.*

than it otherwise would be able to do. Contrary to the conventional wisdom, the principal purpose of trade is to obtain imports, not to hand over exports. Exports are the means to obtain imports, not the other way around. Imports enhance the economy's capabilities, while exports diminish them. Consequently, an export "surplus" actually depletes an economy's strength, while an import surplus (trade deficit) increases it. Although it is true that the U.S. trade deficit cannot and will not go on forever, it is surely not unusual for worthwhile and beneficial circumstances to be of finite duration.

Second, the U.S. trade deficit has arisen not because U.S. exports have fallen, but rather because U.S. imports have risen very substantially. That U.S. exports can and do compete effectively in foreign markets is indicated by the fact that, between 1983 and 1985, U.S. exports increased from $200 billion to about $220 billion at the same time as the trade deficit was rising from $62 billion to over $130 billion.

Of course, the explanation for the increased trade deficit is the sharp rise in U.S. imports: from $263 billion in 1983 to about $350 billion in 1985. It is no doubt true that U.S. exports could increase considerably more than they have if the protective trade practices of other countries were liberalized, and if and as the dollar's exchange value is somewhat reduced. Nevertheless, it still makes far better sense to view the U.S. trade deficit—for good or for ill—as due to the insufficient ability of U.S. domestic production to compete effectively with *imports* within the U.S. market, rather than to the inability of our exports to compete in foreign markets.

Third, inasmuch as substantial real economic growth has been sustained in the United States during the past few years, notwithstanding the increased trade deficit, protectionism can hardly be advocated as necessary to "protect" or "defend" the U.S. recovery. On the contrary, since, as noted above, the deficit itself provides substantial benefits to the U.S. economy, advocates of protectionism in the United States should realize that their advocacy actually amounts not to a defense of the recovery, but rather to an *attack* on consumers and investors.

Finally, while it's true that larger exports generally contribute to more jobs (although in certain instances that's not necessarily so), it is no less true that expanded imports also contribute to more jobs: for example, in the processing and fabrication of imported raw materials and unfinished goods, and in the packaging, distribution, marketing, and servicing of end products. Moreover, the capital inflow that counterbalances the trade and current account deficits plainly adds to jobs through the added domestic investment that is thereby financed. The bottom line, of course, is that the U.S. economy has in fact been an employment engine compared with the economies of Western Europe and even Japan. U.S. civilian employment increased by 7 million jobs between 1983 and 1985, while the trade deficit was growing from $62 to over $130 billion.

"Economics," it has been remarked, "is common sense made difficult." Much of the recent public discussion of the U.S. trade deficit suggests a different relationship: Namely, faulty economics impedes common sense, while good economics (plus a few facts) can help it.

Postaudit

The U.S. economy, currently (in mid-1990) in its ninety-first month of sustained economic expansion, has increased employment by an additional 12 million jobs since 1985, while the trade deficit has fallen to an annual rate of about $100 million (about $80 million in constant 1985 dollars), compared with the $130 billion figure cited in the article.

Unfortunately, the nonsense that has been written about the U.S. trade deficit has not abated since my 1985 article.

37

What's Good about the
Trade Deficit?

Many economists and economic scribes have arrived at a surprising degree of consensus about a particular paradigm to describe recent problems of the U.S. economy. The consensus is surprising because the paradigm itself is seriously flawed.

The paradigm consists of four propositions: (1) government deficits are responsible for high interest rates, (2) high interest rates are responsible for the "overvalued" dollar, (3) the overvalued dollar is responsible for the huge increase in the U.S. trade deficit, and (4) the trade deficit is just plain bad.

The validity of the propositions is limited and decreases as one moves down the list.

Consider the first proposition. As Treasury Secretary Regan often observed, empirical analysis shows no statistically significant historical relationship between budget deficits and interest rates. Over the 1983 to 1984 period, while the deficit more than tripled the prime rate of interest fell from 18.9 to 11 percent. Adjusting interest rates for inflation to approximate the "real" rate of interest doesn't change the picture very much: During the same period the real rate fell from 10 to 7 percent, notwithstanding the tripled deficit.

Nevertheless, there is commonsense validity to the notion that larger government borrowing will, other things being equal, exert upward pressure on interest rates. (However, one point that's usually neglected by those who advance this argument is that efforts to reduce the deficit by increasing taxes may also exert upward pressure on interest rates because increased taxes will result in decreased private savings, rather than simply in reduced private spending.)

A slightly abbreviated version of this essay was published under the title "Reigning Wisdom's Shaky Economic Ground" by the Wall Street Journal *on March 14, 1984.*

Next, consider the proposition about high interest rates as the principal explanation for appreciation of the dollar. Between 1981 and 1984, the dollar's exchange value rose by about 23 percent relative to a trade-weighted average of other currencies. Doubtless high U.S. interest rates relative to those prevailing abroad were partly responsible for the preference of holders of foreign assets to exchange them for dollars. But it is equally certain that high interest rates were only one among several explanations. Other contributory factors include: (1) the relative attractiveness of equity investment and direct investment in U.S. businesses whose sales, profits, and market values have been expected by foreign investors to rise with continued progress of the American recovery; (2) the relatively lower prices of real property even in such premium U.S. markets as New York and Los Angeles compared with Paris, London, and Tokyo; (3) the demand by foreign debtor countries for dollars to help service their dollar debts, thereby resulting in a move by these countries from nondollar to dollar assets; and (4) the relative immunity from political risk of assets held in the United States compared with holdings in other countries.

These four factors, together with high U.S. interest rates, contributed to appreciation of the dollar by increasing the demand for dollar assets among holders of foreign assets. The dollar is in this respect just like a commodity: When demand for it rises, its "price" will increase in terms of other currencies. So the effect of these several influences have been to raise the dollar's price. How the five factors rate in terms of their relative influence on the exchange rate of the dollar is not a matter of knowledge, but of conjecture sometimes slanted by the commentator's political partisanship. Moreover, their relative strength has surely varied substantially at different times in recent years. It is thus remarkable how frequently the dollar's appreciation is attributed to high interest rates alone.

What about the third link in the reasoning chain, that the appreciation or "overvaluation" of the dollar is primarily responsible for the large and growing U.S. trade deficit? In 1983, the U.S. trade deficit rose to $70 billion compared with $43 billion in 1982—an increase of 60 percent in current prices. According to the standard paradigm, appreciation of the dollar is the cause of the increased deficit. Why? Because overvaluation of the dollar, like a tax on exports, raises the prices charged in foreign currencies for U.S.

exports, thereby tending to reduce these exports.   Also, so the argument goes, overvaluation acts like a subsidy on U.S. imports because it enables foreign exporters to charge lower dollar prices and still make a profit on costs they have incurred in their own domestic currencies.

Once again, the argument has partial, but limited, validity. The principal explanation for the increased U.S. trade deficit in the early 1980s is the rapid pace of the U.S. economic recovery, which resulted in a rate of real growth in the GNP of over 6 percent in 1983—more than twice the rate in most of the other countries in the Organization for Economic Cooperation and Development. This, rather than the dollar's appreciation, is the main reason for the 6 percent increase in U.S. *imports*, from $254 billion in 1982 to $269 billion in 1983, because the responsiveness of U.S. imports to increases in our national income is greater than the responsiveness of import to lowered prices.   (In economists' jargon, the income elasticity of demand for imports is greater than their price elasticity.)

The rapid rate of economic growth in the United States also contributed to the reduction of U.S. *exports* of about 5 percent, from $212 billion in 1982 to $200 billion in 1983. When domestic demand grows rapidly, and production capacity is strained in the short run, producers typically tend to satisfy domestic demand rather than potential foreign demand. As a result, exports suffer.

Still another major factor accounting for the reduction of U.S. exports in 1983 was the sharp decrease in U.S. bank lending to developing countries, especially in Latin America.   Such lending, even when not strictly "tied" to U.S. exports, usually facilitates and encourages U.S. exports to the borrowing countries. Diminished U.S. lending accounts to a very considerable extent for the shift during the 1981 to 1983 period in the U.S. trade balance with Latin America's eight largest debtor countries from a $5.8 billion surplus to a $14.5 billion deficit—a swing of over $20 billion. This alone explains almost two thirds of the total increase in the U.S. trade deficit in that period.

Thus, multiple factors besides appreciation of the dollar have contributed significantly to the large U.S. trade deficit.

Finally, how bad is the current and pending U.S. trade deficit? The answer is that there are both positive and negative entries on the ledger.

On the negative side, the trade deficit means reduced employment in the U.S. export sector. Yet even this does not warrant the glib generalizations and loose estimates that have been made about "lost" jobs resulting from the trade deficit. Such estimates overlook the fact that foreign capital inflow, which on the one hand contributes to the trade deficit by raising the exchange value of the dollar, results on the other hand in creating jobs for U.S. workers in manufacturing, housing, and capital goods industries. Whether such capital inflow takes the form of acquiring corporate bonds or equities, or direct investment, or government bonds, it contributes to financing business plant and equipment, construction, or consumer or government spending. Jobs lost in the export sector are thus counterbalanced by jobs gained in other sectors. And there is no particular reason to believe that the "labor intensiveness" of the export sector (reckoned in jobs per dollar of exports) is any greater than the labor intensiveness of the sectors benefiting from foreign capital inflows. The "jobs lost" argument is partly valid, but largely exaggeration.

On the positive side of the ledger, increased exports from the European countries to the United States are a stimulus to their recovery. In effect, the U.S. trade deficit acts as a transmitter of the U.S. recovery abroad. And Europe's recovery is of benefit to the world economy, and surely to the foundations of the Western alliance.

Moreover, a U.S. trade deficit with either or both Europe and the principal debtor countries of Latin America is virtually essential if these countries are to earn the dollar surpluses necessary for servicing and at least partially repaying their hugh dollar debts. Hence, the U.S. trade deficit mitigates, rather than complicates, the world's current financial predicament.

Finally, the trade deficit in itself helps to ease inflationary pressures in the economy (whereas a trade surplus adds to them), and higher imports themselves reflect consumer preferences and contribute to consumer well-being.

There is thus more to be said in favor of the trade deficit than against it.

In sum, the familiar economic paradigm is no stronger than the weakest of its four linked propositions. And all of them are vulnerable.

Postaudit

In retrospect, I wouldn't change a word of this account!

38

A Nonprotectionist Case for
Less Foreign Trade

Right-thinking people generally agree on certain basic propositions about international trade: for example, trade is good; more trade is better than less; and exports are better than imports. The agreement extends, with only rare exceptions, to all parts of the political spectrum, to both sides of the Atlantic, and to the Third World as well as the other two.

This is another example of conventional wisdom concealing palpable unwisdom. In fact, each of the foregoing propositions about trade is either arguable or simply wrong.

The view that trade is good is based on the intuitively appealing notion that *both* parties to a transaction must benefit or else the transaction would not occur. On the contrary, the *countries* involved in the transaction may lose even while the immediate *parties* benefit. This will be true if, as is often the case, the exporter receives a subsidy from government, and hence the price charged may be less than the true costs of production; or, less often, if the importer receives a government subsidy (for example, to encourage some particular type of favored imports, such as high-technology products), and hence the country's real economic costs may be higher than the price actually paid by the importer. Genuine gains from trade result only if the trade occurs without subsidies.

That *more* trade may *not* be better than less trade follows from the same point. If transactions are subsidized, increased trade will only mean greater subsidies, higher real costs, and a larger waste of resources in the subsidizing economies.

A slightly abbreviated version of this essay was published under the title "Less Trade May Be Better Than More" by the Los Angeles Times *on April 28, 1983.*

Finally, the belief that exports are better for the economy than imports is simply wrong. The performance of an economy is in general reflected by the consumption and investment it can sustain. More of both are better than less, and growth in either is better than none. Imports provide additional resources that *contribute* to meeting consumption or investment demands, while exports *subtract* resources from what's available to meet these demands. Hence, in this sense, imports are better than exports. Exports simply provide a means of paying for imports.

Misunderstandings about these points have contributed to the international financial predicament in which the world economy now finds itself, as well as to innumerable other policy mistakes and acts of mischief in the international economy.

In the past several decades, governments in the industrial countries have installed a pervasive network of subsidies designed to promote foreign trade, especially exports. These have taken many forms: export credits, extended on preferential interest and repayment terms; longer-term loan guarantees, intended to make risky loans riskless to the lender and to enable borrowers to increase their imports, usually from the lending country; preferential tax treatment of income derived from foreign sales; and various other means to allow or encourage producers to charge lower prices for exports than for domestic sales.

The tremendous increase in international lending in the 1970s, to both the developing countries and to the countries of Eastern Europe, is partly due to these same misconceptions. The petrodollar surpluses of the 1970s were recycled abroad in part due to a general belief that doing so would result in expanded exports for the recyclers. In hindsight, it is entirely plausible that the world economy as a whole would be better off if more of these resources had been directed toward the domestic economies of the developed countries in accord with more accurate consideration of comparative costs and risks, rather than diverted to Eastern Europe and the less developed countries due to the distortions introduced by trade subsidies.

What is the bottom line?

From the standpoint of public understanding, congressional deliberations, and media attention, it should not be assumed that foreign trade is good in itself and hence deserving of special subsidies or protection.

From the standpoint of public policy, international trade negotiations—between the United States and Japan, the United States and the countries of Western Europe, and among countries taking part in the General Agreement on Tariffs and Trade and other international forums—should move beyond the traditional agenda of tariffs and nontariff barriers.   Instead, more attention should be devoted to identifying and gradually eliminating the pervasive network of hidden and overt subsidies to foreign trade that virtually all of the industrialized countries maintain.

How much of an effect would the multilateral elimination of subsidies have on U.S. foreign trade?   In 1982, U.S. merchandise exports were $212 billion and imports were $244 billion, together representing 14.9 percent of the GNP.   Multilateral elimination of subsidies, negotiated between the United States and its principal trading partners, might reduce these figures by perhaps 10 to 20 percent.   Taxpayers, the general public, and world economic growth would be the beneficiaries of such a reorientation.

Postaudit

There is one qualification I would add to this discussion seven years later.   Where governments in developing countries seek to promote "infant" industries, a convincing case can be made that some form of subsidy for export industries is preferable to protection of import-substituting ones.   In the former instance, the emerging infant is obliged to pass a market test of product quality, which may be (and typically has been) precluded by restrictions on competing imports.

This is one of the lessons of the dramatically successful economic performance of South Korea and Taiwan in the 1980s.

39

Clearing the Haze
Around International Debt

Despite the widespread concern about international debt, most of its essentials have been ignored or obscured.

One neglected point is that the *real* costs, as distinct from the accounting costs, of the $700 billion owed by the developing countries and Eastern Europe *have already been incurred.* These costs are the goods and services, the commodities and machinery, already exported to the debtor countries by the creditors. The real costs are the benefits forgone by the creditors (principally but not exclusively by the United States) because their factors of production—labor, capital, and materials—were used for the benefit of external borrowers rather than for internal investment, research and development, and consumption in the lending countries themselves.

Consider, for example, how much higher *current* U.S. productivity would be if a significant share of the 1970s loans to Latin America had instead financed new investment and R&D in the United States, or if Western European loans to the Soviet Union and Eastern Europe had instead financed investment and R&D within the European Economic Community.

If the real costs of these loans are already "sunk," why all the hullabaloo about the debt?

The hullabaloo revolves around a dilemma: how to maximize repayment of the expended loans without jeopardizing political stability in the debtor countries. Bankers are principally concerned with the first horn of this dilemma, governments in both the creditor and debtor countries principally with the second. And no one really knows how best to reconcile the two.

A slightly abbreviated version of this essay was published under the title "Foreign Loans: At Issue Is Who Bears the Cost?" by the Los Angeles Times *on September 9, 1984.*

One view is that repayment will be maximized by providing additional funds to the debtors to help get their economic houses in order—to maintain essential imports, reduce inflation without severely curtailing consumption or precipitating acute deflation, boost output and exports, and thereby be better able to service prior debts as well as new loans. According to this view, new loans are also necessary to avoid the serious political instability that might result in the debtor countries if their imports, consumption, and output were to decline further, absent the new financing. For example, nascent democracy in Argentina might be severely jeopardized as a result.

Based on this reasoning, most governments in both creditor and debtor countries favor some form of new lending, subsidized by government underwriting of commercial lending, additions to the concessional lending pool of the International Monetary Fund, or other means.

A sharply different view is that the necessary economic housekeeping by the debtors depends on their own efforts to reallocate resources from consumption to investment and exports. Since the necessary resource shifts are only about 4 or 5 percent of the debtors' GNPs, political stability isn't likely to be significantly affected. If these reallocation efforts are genuine and promising, it is argued, the debtors will be able to service their debt and regain normal access to international capital markets fairly soon. If, on the other hand, their efforts are not promising, then any new lending would simply be throwing good money after bad.

This position runs the risk that the debtors—at least the most severely beleaguered ones—may simply default, as Bolivia has already done. Even so, it can be argued, the defaulting debtors will be obliged to repay eventually in order to regain access to international capital markets. Hence, the argument runs, the creditors will recover more of what they're owed anyhow, without having incurred the added costs of new lending.

In between these two positions lie numerous possible compromises to reconcile the various conflicting aims. Proposals to reschedule existing debts, to place an arbitrary cap on interest rates charged to debtors, to confine debt service to a specified amount while allowing maturities to vary, to swap debt for equity in the debtor countries, or to provide new loans through the IMF, are the elements of these compromises. Such proposals for concessions by creditors would entail various conditions to be accepted by the debtors.

Whatever the compromises that emerge—and they're likely to differ for different countries—there's little doubt that the ensuing repayments will be worth substantially less than the original loans. So the ultimate issue—indeed, the haziest part of the international debt predicament—is how this loss is to be divided among bank management, bank stockholders, depositors, and governments (which is to say, the public). Whose balance sheet will suffer and by how much?

Except for the bankers, most observers at least tacitly agree that the burden should be principally borne by bank management and stockholders, with depositors held harmless, and taxpayers as the burden-carrier of last resort. Because management and stockholders have previously realized gains from increases in bank earnings, it is appropriate that they should incur losses when these earnings decline.

It's equally appropriate that depositors should be protected, both because of the special fiduciary character of the banks' relation to their individual depositors (in contrast to their stockholders), and also because insolvency in the major banks could have serious systemic repercussions because the smaller regional banks hold deposits in the major international ones. Protection of depositors is already implied by the Federal Deposit Insurance Corporation's speedy intervention in the Continental Illinois debacle earlier this year.

But protecting depositors means that the general public is likely to bear part of the burden. The reason is that losses from the original loans may be so great that not only will bank earnings decline further (from nonaccrual of interest payments) but the portfolio value of many of these international loans will be sharply reduced as well. The net losses may well be sufficiently large that, to avoid insolvency of some of the major banks and thus protect depositors, the Federal Reserve may have to stand as a lender of last resort. This safety net implies that the Fed would be willing to make loans on the banks' discounted assets in amounts sufficient to preserve solvency—that is, a positive net worth—of the threatened banks. And this is where the taxpayers' burden arises. Lending by the Fed to relieve or reduce the banks' exposure to their soured loans ultimately represents a claim on the earnings and savings of the public at large.

If this is the bad news, the good news is that such action by the Federal Reserve needn't cause concern about triggering inflation.

Increases in the reserves of some banks due to such action by the Fed can be fully or partly offset for the banking system as a whole by open market operations (Fed sales of government securities to the unaffected banks) designed to keep the money supply within the established target range. One alternative to Fed involvement lies in a U.S. decision to provide additional capital for IMF lending to the beleaguered debtors. In this case, taxpayers would bear the burden more directly, because these funds would have to come from U.S. tax revenues.

When the dust settles, effective management of the debt predicament can be partly judged by the extent to which the imposed burden on the public has been kept within limited bounds.

Postaudit

Since the article was written in 1984, the nominal debt of the less developed countries and Eastern Europe has risen to well over $1 trillion, as a result of rollovers, rescheduling, and illusory "new" lending to enable the fiction of debt service to be maintained. The various debt relief proposals associated with the Baker, Brady, and Miyazawa plans have been notably unsuccessful in relieving the nominal debt problem.

It is perhaps time to consider something as drastic as an agreement to settle this accumulated debt on the basis of some substantial markdown of principal—perhaps based on prevailing discounts in the secondary debt market, and with a larger markdown of commercial bank debt and a smaller one on sovereign intergovernment debt.

40

Who Owes Whom, and How Much?

Coauthored with Sarah Holden

That the United States is the world's largest debtor has, by now, become a commonplace. The basis for this belief is the official Department of Commerce report that the full accounting of international assets and liabilities of the United States showed a net negative balance of $264 billion at the end of 1986.

Despite the pervasiveness of this belief, and the general acceptance of the underlying data, both the belief and the data are mistaken. The basic error arises from a failure to apply a proper economic valuation to all, rather than to only some, of the various components in the full international balance sheet of the United States. When the appropriate valuation methodology is applied to all of the components, the full balance position of the United States at the end of 1986 turns out to have been a positive $50 billion, rather than a negative $264 billion!

Lest this surprising conclusion suggests greater precision than is warranted, it should be plainly acknowledged that there remain many uncertainties and ambiguities in the underlying data. However, this caveat applies even more strongly to the original negative ("debtor") figure than to our revised and positive ("creditor") one.

For a proper economic valuation to be made of the U.S. international balance sheet, each of the principal components of the balance should be "market-to-market"—that is, evaluated at its current market value, as best this can be estimated. Of course that is easier said than done, and it is admittedly more difficult to do for some components than for others. Still, the effort should be made for *all* of the components rather than for only those that seem easy to do.

A slightly abbreviated version of this essay was published in the Wall Street Journal *on January 6, 1988.*

The official estimates that have been made assess at their estimated current market value only securities holdings (by both foreign holders of U.S. securities and U.S. holders of foreign securities). The other major components typically included in the international balance calculations—direct investment (including reinvested earnings net of depreciation), government loans, bank and nonbank claims, and official gold holdings—are misleadingly valued at their book or nominal values, in the official figures—clearly an erroneous procedure.

While this accounting practice is convenient, it introduces three principal and substantial sources of error.

First, the resulting underestimate of U.S. direct investment abroad is much larger than the underestimate of foreign direct investment in the United States. The reason is that direct investments by U.S. corporations abroad, including their reinvestment of earnings net of depreciation, are generally of older vintage than the corresponding investments by foreign corporations in the United States. Consequently, the respective book valuations of U.S. direct investments reflect the much lower costs and prices prevailing when the U.S. investments were made, while the more recent direct investments in the United States by foreign corporations occurred at costs and prices closer to currently prevailing ones. Therefore, if U.S. investments abroad, and foreign direct investments in the United States, are converted from their book values at original cost into 1986 dollars to arrive at a closer approximation of their true market value, the result is a net increase in the value of U.S. holdings of about $260 billion above a similar valuation of foreign direct investments in the United States.

Second, the book or nominal value of loans owed to U.S. banks and nonbanking institutions by the principal developing countries is plainly a substantial *overestimate* of their true market value. A closer approximation of the market value of these claims, based on averaging the currently prevailing discounts in the secondary debt market, results in *reducing* the net value of these loans at the end of 1986 by approximately $38 billion.

Finally, the official estimates of the net international position of the United States includes U.S. gold reserves valued at the "official" gold price of $42 per ounce, rather than the prevailing market price of gold. Marking the gold reserves to a market valuation results in an *upward* adjustment of about $91 billion in the U.S. asset position.

As noted earlier, the combined effect of these three adjustments is to shift the resulting balance from a large negative figure ($264 billion) at the end of 1986, to a small positive figure ($50 billion).

It's important to note that this conclusion is also corroborated by the fact that, in 1986, the U.S. balance of payments showed *net* investment income of $21 billion, representing the excess of remitted profits, dividends, and interest derived from U.S. holdings abroad over the corresponding earnings from foreign holdings in the United States.

Although our recalculation is probably closer to being accurate than the commonly accepted estimates, its significance shouldn't be exaggerated. As noted earlier, the underlying data are neither complete nor wholly reliable. Other problems also arise, for example, in connection with the appropriate way to treat the assets and liabilities of foreign subsidiaries of U.S. banks, and of the U.S. subsidiaries of foreign banks, and how to handle the valuation of "sovereign" debt owed to U.S. government institutions. Indeed, depending on how one handles these matters, as well as the recurring errors and omissions in the U.S. balance of payments, a wide range of estimates of the U.S. international position can be generated.

To be sure, even if the United States was, in fact, a net creditor at the end of 1986, it will probably shift to a debtor position by the end of 1987, because of an expected U.S. trade deficit in 1987 of over $165 billion. Actually, even this prediction is uncertain. As a result of "Black Monday," the 1987 market value of foreign holdings of U.S. securities will be reduced by substantially more than the corresponding reduction of U.S. holdings abroad. Moreover, the market price of gold in 1987 has increased about 30 percent above that in 1986, thus warranting a corresponding increase in that component of the full international balance sheet of the United States.

If, nevertheless, the actual debtor status of the United States lies sometime in the future rather than in the past, the burden of servicing such potential net foreign assetholdings in the United States will be that much lower than has hitherto been assumed. Furthermore, beliefs about the U.S. international financial position may sometimes affect behavior; hence, dispelling erroneous ones can be useful, especially where the erroneous beliefs have been as widely held and as highly publicized as those relating to the international financial position of the United States.

Postaudit

Once again, contrary to the conventional unwisdom, it is not clear in 1990 whether the real market value of U.S. holdings of foreign assets is greater or less than foreign holdings of U.S. assets. (In calendar year 1988, the United States had a small excess of remitted earnings from its holdings abroad over the corresponding earnings from foreign holdings in the United States.) More to the point is the fact that, whether this figure is positive or negative, it signifies remarkably little about the economic vigor and prospects of the American economy.

41

The Missing Chapter in the International Debt Story

Among the four largest debtor countries in the Third World, one (Korea) currently commands an A-1 credit rating in world capital markets, enabling it to borrow amply at rates equal to the best available to any borrower in those markets. The other three (Argentina, Brazil, and Mexico) can borrow only by pleading with new creditors, or by coercing old ones using the explicit or implicit threat of default as the stick. In either case, the A-B-M (Argentina-Brazil-Mexico) countries are obliged to accept restrictive conditions, as well as interest rates and other terms that reflect the extra risk that lending to them is believed to entail. As an indication of this perceived risk, the existing debts of Mexico, Argentina, and Brazil trade on the secondary debt market at discounts of 38, 33, and 24 percent, respectively. By contrast, the existing debt of Korea is worth at least a hundred cents on the dollar.

Among the four countries, Brazil's and Mexico's total debts are the largest ($108 billion and $100 billion, respectively), Korea is next ($52 billion), and Argentina is fourth ($50 billion). As a group, the four account for more than half of total Third World debt.

What explains the striking differences in the credit standing of the four? The contributing explanations include several that are familiar, and one that is much less familiar and certainly less publicized but which is probably of still greater importance than the others. Moreover, the less familiar one carries with it major, as well as neglected, policy significance.

The familiar explanations relate to the fact that Korea has been and is a rapidly growing (7.5 percent in 1986) economy, with booming

---

A slightly abbreviated version of this essay was published under the title "Missing Chapter in Third World Debt" in the Wall Street Journal *on March 19, 1987.*

export industries, a manageable debt service ratio (about 15 percent), and a rapidly rising inflow of direct and equity investment from abroad.

By contrast, Argentina, Brazil, and Mexico are experiencing slow or no aggregate economic growth, limited export growth in relation to their massive debt burdens, and a dearth of foreign capital inflow.

The less familiar explanation lies in the sharply contrasting history of capital flight in the three poor credit risks (Mexico, Argentina, and Brazil) on the one hand, and the strongly rated fourth one (Korea), on the other. To a very substantial degree, the prior debt accumulated by the A-B-M countries simply financed capital flight from those countries, whereas nearly all of Korea's prior debt contributed directly or indirectly to capital formation and to increased production and export capacity; it is the latter that has provided the solid foundation for Korea's current strong credit rating and competitive position in world markets.

Between 1976 and 1985, cumulative capital outflows from Argentina and Mexico represented more than 50 percent of their total accumulated debt. The corresponding capital flight figure for Brazil has been estimated at between 10 and 18 percent of its total debt, but this is probably an underestimate. In other words, for the three A-B-M countries, capital flight—accomplished by whatever direct or indirect means—amounted to about $95 billion of their collective debt of $260 billion. In effect, 35 percent of these countries' total borrowings was directly nullified by acquisition of foreign assets by their own citizens and other nonbank institutions. So-called "sovereign debt" was thus incurred by the three governments in exchange for assets acquired by private citizens or institutions of their respective countries.

This situation has a direct bearing on the predicament in which these and other Third World debtors currently find themselves, on the dubious wisdom of most recent plans and proposals that seek to improve matters, and on finding a more promising approach to resolving the debt problem.

If and as the enormous 1975 to 1985 flight of capital from Argentina, Brazil, and Mexico is reversed, their demands for further borrowing will be reduced, their access to it will be eased, and the economic effectiveness of their subsequent borrowing will be enhanced. On the other hand, unless and until such capital repatriation occurs, there is every reason to expect that further borrowing will to a considerable extent be nullified by further capital flight. Even with the existence of tighter exchange controls in the three countries, new borrowing can be converted into new capital flight in various ways; for example, by overinvoicing of imports, underinvoicing of exports, and other adroit measures designed to circumvent the controls.

An important conclusion follows: Efforts to ease the Third World debt problem should focus on the conditions that promote and provoke capital flight and on the conditions that will induce capital to return. These conditions relate to political stability and the predictability of the political environment, tax and monetary policies, labor and wage legislation, regulatory policies, and the general political and administrative climate for investment—whether by repatriated "old" capital or by new internal or foreign capital. If and as progress is realized in improving these conditions, less new borrowing will be needed, and the burden of servicing existing debt will be eased. In the absence of such progress, new loans will be wasted and the burden of outstanding debt will simply be magnified, thereby further dimming prospects of repayment.

Postaudit

In the three intervening years since this piece was written, Korea's holdings of foreign assets have begun to approach, if not yet exceed, foreign asset holdings in Korea. On the other hand, the foreign debts of Brazil, Mexico, and Argentina have increased as a result of rollovers and nominal new lending to cover previous debt service obligations (see the Postaudit in chap. 39). The central thrust of the article seems to me entirely valid three years later.

42

The Dollar's Impending Climb

At the beginning of 1986, the U.S. dollar exchanged for 200 Japanese yen. Toward the end of 1987, the dollar's exchange rate was about 140 yen.

In the next six to twelve months, the dollar's value relative to the yen is, I believe, more likely to rise appreciably than to fall or stay where it presently is—a forecast that runs against much of the current conventional wisdom.

To place this forecast in perspective, it's worth noting that the U.S. global trade deficit (goods and services) in 1986 was $135 billion, and the bilateral deficit with Japan was about half this total. In 1987, the global deficit will probably be in the neighborhood of $150, of which about $80 billion will consist of the bilateral deficit with Japan.

What lies behind this forecast of a climb in the dollar's value are several factors that will increase international demand for dollars by holders of yen, and reduce the supply of dollars for making international payments in yen. When the demand for something rises and its supply declines, the result is an increase in its price—in this case, the price or exchange value of the dollar.

The demand for dollars by holders of yen will tend to rise for two reasons. First, the price/earnings ratios prevailing in Japanese stock markets are three or four times those prevailing in U.S. markets. (Even allowing for foreign exchange risks, this relative inflation of Japanese P/E ratios will make U.S. equities look especially attractive to holders of yen assets.) Second, real property values in Tokyo and other major Japanese cities are similarly inflated relative to land prices in U.S. urban areas (land prices in Tokyo rose by 200 percent in the 1985 to 1987 period), thereby making acquisition of U.S. real

---

An abbreviated version of this essay was published under the title "Some Signs of an Upturn For a Well-Battered Dollar" in the Los Angeles Times *on September 6, 1987.*

property increasingly attractive to Japanese real estate investors and developers.

The prospective reduction in the supply of dollars for making international payments to Japan is likely to come about primarily through domestic U.S. production substituting for some imports, and secondarily from increased U.S. exports. Both of these developments are likely to result, if somewhat belatedly, from the depreciation of the dollar relative to the yen that has already occurred, together with the rise in Japan's real labor costs relative to those in the United States. These two effects will make U.S. products more competitive with those from Japan, especially in the U.S. market and, perhaps with some delay, in the Japanese market as well.

Finally, one additional factor will contribute to a further strengthening of the dollar. The Federal Reserve Board's new chairman, Alan Greenspan, is likely to maintain at least as tight a monetary policy as Paul Volcker would have done, for various reasons, including a desire to demonstrate to the markets that his anti-inflationary commitment is not less than what in Volcker's case would have been taken for granted. Somewhat higher real interest rates in the United States will make U.S. debt instruments more attractive to foreign assetholders.

Of course, all of this still falls short of an unqualified, iron-clad prediction. To be sure, counterarguments and influences can be cited that may offset some of these tendencies. For example, government spending may be boosted in an election year, resulting in reversing the downward trend in the federal budget deficit; or U.S. private savings might decline further and consumer spending might reignite, thereby generating increased demand for Japanese as well as other imports. However, the tendencies mentioned earlier add up to a much stronger case for anticipating an appreciation than a depreciation of the dollar in the forthcoming months.

Macroeconomics is not so much a dismal science as simply a profoundly uncertain one. As someone once said, "Half of what we know about macroeconomics is wrong, and the trouble is we're not quite sure which half."

Postaudit

I was plainly wrong on this one!   The dollar remained weak through 1988.   Its rise (by about 15 percent) occurred in the second half of 1989, too remote from my mildly hedged forecast to be considered as other than erroneous.

43

A Vote of Confidence in Los Angeles

On the premise that Japanese investors are generally shrewd, their enormous holdings of prime commercial property in Los Angeles should be viewed by Angelenos as encouraging and reassuring. Commercial property is a long-term—as well as a relatively illiquid—asset, so investors who acquire and hold it evidently expect the local economy's future to be bright. Presumably such expectations underlie the remarkable growth in recent years of Japanese property holdings in Los Angeles as well as in several other major metropolitan areas, including Honolulu, San Francisco, and New York.

At the end of 1986, Japanese firms and institutional investors owned 16 of the 32 largest commercial buildings and major building sites held by foreign investors in the prime business area of downtown Los Angeles. At the end of 1987, the corresponding figures were 24 of 40. The total investment represented by these Japanese holdings approaches $2.5 billion. In the aggregate, these holdings make up about 30 percent of the prime commercial property in downtown Los Angeles.

Some people view this phenomenon as disquieting, or even alarming, rather than reassuring. Instead of seeing the Japanese position as an encouraging indicator that the Los Angeles economy's prospects are bright, they worry that it may foretell an excessive degree of Japanese economic leverage, as well as an effort by the Japanese to acquire and exercise economic influence in a somewhat devious way.

The worriers are wrong. Japanese acquisition of commercial property is a legitimate, sound, healthy reflection of the manifest strengths—as well as some of the weaknesses—of the U.S. economy.

A slightly abbreviated version of this essay was published in the Los Angeles Times *on June 17, 1988.*

Japanese property acquisition is a specific example of increased Japanese holdings of U.S. assets of all types—including government and corporate bonds, equities, and direct investment in plant and equipment—currently making up a total asset pool worth more than $250 billion.

While these holdings are enormous, they should be placed in proper context. The aggregate value of all U.S. tangible assets is probably well over $15 trillion. Japanese holdings are therefore perhaps 1.6 percent of the total.

In economic terms, Japanese holdings of U.S. assets in general, and of Los Angeles real estate in particular, have resulted from a process of voluntary exchange: The United States imports more than it exports (that is our trade deficit with Japan) while Japan buys more U.S. assets than it sells Japanese assets to Americans. This voluntary exchange results because, under present circumstances, U.S. citizens and corporations choose to import more from Japan than they export, while Japanese citizens and corporations find more attractive opportunities for investing in the United States than they find at home.

As with all voluntary exchanges, presumably both parties benefit. For the United States the result has been higher levels of investment and consumption than would otherwise have occurred, and the generally impressive performance of the American economy in recent years: sustained economic growth over the past five and a half years, the longest period of uninterrupted peacetime growth in this century; increased employment amounting to 16 million jobs in the past seven years; the lowest unemployment rate (5.5 percent) since 1979; and reasonable price stability since 1982.

For Japan the result also has been sustained economic growth, slowly rising levels of consumption, and its emergence as the world's largest creditor nation.

Japanese property acquisition in Los Angeles has contributed to increased construction, higher employment, and improved business office facilities.

If the United States wants to alter this pattern of voluntary and mutually beneficial exchange—that is to say, the sale of U.S. property and other assets to compensate for our large, though gradually declining trade deficits—we have it in our power to do so. We simply have to spend somewhat less, save somewhat more, and invest the difference. This can be accomplished in various ways: an added tax on consumption (Japan, as well as virtually all developed countries, levies much heavier consumption taxes than we do, and in particular, much heavier taxes on gasoline); allowing for the partial tax deductibility of saved income (Japan's tax system provides many more extensive incentives for savings than did our now-repeated IRA and Keogh plans); and continuing pressure on our Japanese trading partners to reduce their restrictions on imports of beef, citrus, and other products while opening further opportunities for sales in Japan of American engineering, construction, information, legal, financial, and other services.

Reshaping the prior pattern of exchange, which has had both quids and quos associated with it, requires a combination of straightforward changes in U.S. domestic policies as well as persistent and tough negotiation with a major and respected ally—one, it should be remembered, that shares fundamental national interests and democratic values with the United States.

Postaudit

Japanese restrictions on U.S. beef and citrus imports have been eased since this was written, but the main themes appear to me as sound now as they were in 1988.

44

The Weaknesses in Japan's Economic Strength

It is standard, as well as fashionable in some quarters, to extol the efficiency and vigor of Japan's economy, and to contrast it disparagingly with the "noncompetitiveness" and torpor of the American economy. But the facts are more complex. The glitter surrounding its strong economic performance in recent years obscures Japan's serious problems, weaknesses, and anachronisms.

One major problem is reflected by a striking anomaly: virtually all goods and services are more expensive in Japan at the 130 yen to the dollar exchange rate than the same or closely substitutable goods and services in the United States. This applies across the board to a wide range of consumer and commercial final demands: nontradables (for example, land, housing, office space, hotel rates); services (cab fares, haircuts, laundry); and tradable commodities (cars, cameras, VCRs, food staples and beverages, shoes, tennis rackets). A survey last year by Japan's Economic Planning Agency found that, for a broad sample of 306 goods and services, prices in Tokyo were between 26 and 48 percent higher than in New York.

In particular, Japanese consumers have been scantily served by Japan's stellar progress and power in the world economy.

Thus, the yen is manifestly overvalued at the present exchange rate, compared to its internal purchasing power. Moreover, the explanation that's usually offered for persistence of an overvalued rate—namely, capital flows—doesn't explain the disparity between the yen's exchange rate and its purchasing power because, in the present instance, the capital flows are in the wrong direction!

A slightly abbreviated version of this essay was published under the title "The Weaknesses Amid Japan's Economic Strengths" in the Wall Street Journal *on May 19, 1989.*

In principal, any of three possible explanations, or combinations among them, can account for this situation.

One explanation relates to trade restrictions, such as Japan's quotas on various agricultural imports, especially rice, beef, citrus products, soybeans, and soy products. As part of the ongoing Uruguay round of the General Agreement on Tariffs and Trade negotiations, the Japanese have evidently agreed to explore an accelerated reduction of these barriers in the coming years. On the other hand, the national sales tax recently passed as a matter of high policy priority by the Japanese government—one of the principal factors responsible for Mr. Takeshita's downfall—moves in exactly the wrong direction, by adding to the disparity between internal and foreign prices of Japanese goods because exports are exempted from the tax while it applies to all domestic sales.

A second explanation relates to the possibility of price discrimination by Japanese firms: namely, charging lower prices in more elastic (that is, more price responsive) foreign markets than in the less elastic domestic market. This is not the same as "dumping" to the extent that dumping implies selling below marginal costs. Nor does the possible practice of price discrimination by Japanese firms necessarily imply that the practice reflects Japanese government policy or intentions. It does, however, carry implications with respect to the possible "coordination" of pricing policy, whether by direct or indirect means, among and by Japanese firms engaged in international trade.

The third explanation relates to the counterintuitive, but empirically probably valid, notion that the cost of distribution and marketing—of moving commodities from manufacturers through the hands of jobbers, middlemen, and wholesalers, to the retailer and eventually to the consumer—may be considerably higher in Japan than they are in foreign markets, and, in particular, than they are in the United States. Japan employs about 15 million people, or 25 percent of its entire labor force, in these intermediary distributional roles, compared to between one fifth and one half that percentage in the United States, depending on whether one defines the comparable U.S. employment figure in terms of wholesale trade alone or inclusive of all sales occupations. Typically, in Japan there are four or five separate commodity handlers, each of whom receives a markup on handling and distribution. And these anachronistic "featherbedding" practices in Japan are protected by licensure requirements at the prefecture rather than at the central government level.

The effect of this hierarchic and anachronistic distribution system is that, from the standpoint of individual firms, the costs of distribution in the U.S. market ten thousand miles away are actually lower than the costs of distribution within the Japanese islands themselves! These higher costs mean higher prices at home and lower prices abroad—just the opposite of what standard theory implies. Thus, the distinctly mercantilist character of the Japanese economy results, in part at least, from the inefficient and obsolete structure of its distribution and marketing system.

Apart from the implications of this third explanation for the well-being of Japanese consumers, the point also carries implications with respect to the world economy and more particularly to U.S. negotiations with its close Japanese ally. If the foregoing analysis is correct, it would seem that we should press the Japanese to remove, or at least to liberalize, these prefecture licensing practices so that large-scale and single-stage distribution and marketing operations can be facilitated in Japan. Encouraging such operations would be helpful to the U.S. balance of payments even if those operations were principally undertaken by Japanese firms rather than by foreign firms. The reason is that if the efforts were successful, the effect would be to lower distribution costs in the Japanese home market so that Japanese firms would find it relatively more attractive to sell at home than abroad, compared with the present situation where the reverse position exists.

Another anachronistic inefficiency in the Japanese economy is its woefully antiquated highway and general infrastructure system. In many respects, this system is more comparable to what one finds in parts of the Third World than what one expects to find in the more developed world. For example, highways are poorly engineered, have narrow lanes, and no road shoulders. Hence, any vehicle that has an accident or that malfunctions in some way, or any emergency that requires ambulances to move through traffic, creates a nearly impenetrable roadblock and results in enormous time delays and serious economic inefficiencies. Modernization of the obsolete Japanese highway and housing infrastructure would entail public and private expenditures of dozens of billions of dollars.

Moreover, there is some evidence that Japanese design and construction services are relatively much higher in costs than comparable, or even superior, services in the United States. If the Japanese were to move rapidly to open government and nongovernment construction and engineering contracting to bidding by foreign construction and engineering firms, it is likely that U.S. firms could become effective competitors in this currently highly restricted Japanese market. The results would benefit Japanese consumers, commuters, and travelers, and would also contribute to reducing Japan's embarrassingly large current account surplus with the United States.

Whether by design or inadvertence—and probably some of both ingredients are involved—Japan's structural economic anachronisms contribute paradoxically to its effective mercantilist performance at the expense of Japanese consumers as well as foreign competitors. Accelerated efforts to overcome and modernize these anachronisms would contribute notably to the well-being of Japanese consumers, to Japan's relations with the United States, and to Japan's standing in the international community.

Postaudit

Many of the issues and arguments advanced in this article have been reflected—whether by cause or coincidence—in the 1990 Strategic Impediments Initiatives (SII) agreements between the United States and Japan.

45

Clouds over Japan's
Economic Future

The Japanese economy, according to the current consensus, is sound and its prospects bullish. According to a recent Gallup poll, twice as many people (58 percent) think Japan is "the world's leading economic power" as accord that position to the United States. When asked to assess the outlook in the year 2000, a plurality of respondents continue to rate Japan ahead of the United States, although the margin falls from two to one currently, to four to three in 2000.

Among most U.S. Japanologists, there is even greater certainty. Their prevailing view is that the Japanese economy will continue to move forward smoothly and successfully, outdistancing the United States and Western Europe in the process.

Views of the American business community are more ambivalent, although many in financial circles express judgments similar to those mentioned above. They cite as corroborative evidence that Japanese corporations listed on the Tokyo Exchange currently represent about 50 percent more in corporate capitalization than all of the U.S. corporations carried on the New York Stock Exchange, and probably will continue to do so!

There are numerous reasons for believing this consensus is wrong. Contrary to prevailing opinion, the Japanese economy faces several significant risks in the years ahead—risks that may well add up to a likely prospect of relative decline in Japan's position in the world economy during the next decade.

One risk is that the Tokyo stock market may crash in the next few years by even more than the 20 percent drop in the New York Exchange in October 1987. The Nikkei index, currently in the 34,000

Published under the title "Crashing Markets, Tumbling Services: Japan in 2000" in the Wall Street Journal on August 3, 1989.

range, has risen eightfold in the past decade, compared to a rise of less than 40 percent of that amount in the Dow index during the same period. This extraordinary rise has propelled price earnings ratios on the Tokyo market to about 55 to 1, compared to about 12 to 1 in the New York market. But the foundation on which the Tokyo market's escalation rests is quite fragile because it is partly based on a contrived scarcity of land in the area environing Tokyo and other major cities. The result has been an extraordinary inflation of urban land prices in recent years—for example, Tokyo land values have risen by 200 percent since 1986—which has inflated the balance sheets and stock prices of large Japanese corporations having major holdings of urban land.

The Tokyo market's foundation is fragile because a large part of the scarcity is contrived rather than real. The contrivance results from zoning restrictions that, while ostensibly protecting farmland from commercial development as a means of boosting domestic rice production and contributing to "food security," actually provide a lucrative asset multiplier for big business owners of urban land. As the Japanese middle class, squeezed as it has been between big business and rice farmers (the domestic price of rice is five or six times the world market price), becomes increasingly politically active—already evident in public reactions to the Recruit scandal, to Mr. Takeshita's ill-advised consumption tax, and to Mr. Uno's personal vagaries—the zoning restrictions are likely to be revised, urban land values will begin to dip, and the Nikkei index and price earnings ratios are likely to tumble.

A second major reason why economic clouds may darken the rising sun relates to Japan's savings rate. In the period from 1979 to 1984, Japan's private savings rate (household savings plus corporate savings as a ratio to private national income) exceeded that of the United States by nearly 11 percentage points (21.4 versus 10.6 percent, respectively), and exceeded the average for countries in the Organization for Economic Cooperation and Development by nearly 7 percent. These large and protracted margins have fueled Japan's export-led growth. They have also financed its investment in advanced technology at home, its accumulation of enormous assets abroad—including over $400 billion in the United States—and its present position as the principal source of capital in global financial markets. According to a meticulous recent study by Professor Charles

Horioka of Osaka University, two thirds of the difference between the Japanese and U.S. savings rates are explained by demographic factors: a lower ratio of the aged (over 64) to the working-age population and a lower ratio of the nonworking young (under 19) to the working-age population. Since these two nonworking, dependent age cohorts are generally not savers, these low ratios in Japan have in the past tended to boost aggregate savings rates relative to those of other economies with higher ratios.

The economic cloud that this portends arises from the fact that, by the year 2000, the ratio of the aged in Japan is expected to rise by 80 percent above the 1975 to 1984 averages (from 15 to 27 percent), while the ratio of the nonworking young to the working-age population will decline by less than 25 percent. The effect of these two variables—the former tending to lower the savings rate and the latter to raise it—will be a net lowering of the aggregate Japanese savings rate by 8.3 percent by 2000, during a period when the U.S. savings rate is likely to stay the same or perhaps to rise from where it has been in recent years.

In addition to the powerful effects of changing demographics, Japanese consumption propensities are also likely to rise across all segments of the population due to their increased exposure to higher living standards and more affluent life-styles in the United States and Western Europe.

As a result of the combined effects of demographic change and shifting social standards, by 2000 Japan is therefore likely to assume the role of a mature creditor country, importing more than it is exporting, and earning more from its foreign assetholdings than it is investing abroad to add to them.

Finally, the deep-seated mercantilist orientation of the Japanese economy will probably be buffeted by two strong forces in the international trade arena. The more familiar one is the prospect of both formal and informal protectionism in the U.S. and European markets. The less familiar but increasingly important one is the displacement of Japanese consumer durable products by competing lines from the newly industrialized economies (NIEs), notably Korea, Taiwan, Singapore, and Hong Kong, both in international markets and in the Japanese home market. Indeed, the prospective, "demercantilizing" of Japanese trade policy, in response to the recommendations of the Miyakawa report and continued pressure from the United States and

Western Europe, is more likely to accelerate penetration of the Japanese market by exports from the NIEs than by those of the United States and Western Europe!

Of course, the clouds over Japan's economic future may dissipate rather than intensify. My own guess is that the second outcome is at least as likely as the first. Although abundant worries have been vociferously expressed in the media and elsewhere in recent years about the impending relative economic decline of the United States, there are probably stronger grounds for anticipating this for Japan than for the United States in the next decade.

Postaudit

I believe this piece was one of the few, if not the only, contemporaneous forecast of a greater than 20 percent drop in the Nikkei index, which actually ensued in the first few months of 1990. The other points in the article are still relevant and timely.

46

How Socialism in Japan May Help Capitalism in the United States

The role of Japan's Socialist Party (JSP) in Japanese politics, and the party's influence on Japanese policies, will probably, if not inevitably, increase in the near future. This may ensue either directly, if the party wins the impending Lower House elections and then forms a new government with its coalition partners; or indirectly, if it becomes a larger and more effective opposition to another Liberal Democratic Party (LDP) government; or more indirectly still, if the LDP, to forestall the Socialists' ascendance, preempts the salient themes espoused by the JSP.

This prospect of increased JSP influence on economic policies in Japan carries with it both good news and bad news for the United States economy and for the international economy as a whole.

The bad news is that the JSP's trade policy stance is actually more protectionist than that of the LDP. The JSP opposed the 1986 Miyakawa Report's wide-ranging proposals for opening the Japanese economy, as well as the 1988 Japanese agreement with the United States to eliminate quotas on Japan's imports of beef and citrus products over the next decade.

But the JSP's increased influence will also entail some beneficial economic consequences and, paradoxically, this good news will probably more than offset the bad in the economic domain. The JSP's influence will probably accelerate Japan's transition toward a better balanced economic structure and, as a consequence, toward a more open and less protectionist international one.

Japan's remarkable economic accomplishments of the past two decades have been based on a quintessentially neomercantilist struc-

---

A slightly abbreviated version of this essay was published in the New York Times *under the title "If Japan's Socialists Gain ..." on November 18, 1989.*

ture characterized by a set of sustained and deliberate imbalances: a sustained excess of domestic savings over domestic investment; a related excess of Japanese exports over imports; a deprivation of public investment in transportation and housing; and a pervasive disparity between the purchasing power value of the yen at home and its foreign exchange value abroad. The disparity between the yen's purchasing power and its foreign exchange value translates into substantially higher prices for virtually all tradable and nontradable goods and services within Japan compared with their prices abroad, to the detriment of the Japanese consumer. A survey last year by Japan's Economic Planning Agency found that, for a broad sample of 306 goods and services, prices in Tokyo were between 26 and 48 percent higher than those in New York.

These imbalances are likely to be moderated if not corrected by the JSP's predilections and policies—whether the changes come about by design or inadvertence.

For example, the party is committed to repeal of the politically unpopular, as well as economically ill-advised, 3 percent consumption tax enacted by the Takeshita government in 1988. The tax is economically ill-advised because it tends to make savings more attractive than consumption—just the opposite of what economic restructuring in Japan should aim for in order to correct the savings-investment imbalance. Related to this change in tax policy, the JSP can be expected to press for a pricing structure that reduces if not eliminates the disparity between domestic and foreign prices by lowering the former, for the benefit of the squeezed Japanese consumer.

Furthermore, the JSP's political priorities are likely to favor increases in government investment, as well as incentives for private investment, to expand production of consumer services in health, housing, and education. The policy orientations of the JSP are also more likely than those of the LDP to lead to increased social welfare expenditures for the aged, disabled, socially or economically disadvantaged, and unemployed. Other potential needs for increased public investment lie in modernization of Japan's antiquated road, highway, and airport infrastructure, as well as improvements in environmental protection and waste disposal. These forms of public investment are at least as likely to be recognized as priority claimants for additional public investment by the JSP as by the LDP.

It is significant that Japan's total central and local government expenditures have typically been the lowest among any of the industrial democracies, averaging less than 25 percent of its GNP during the 1980s, compared with about 36 percent for the United States and nearly 50 percent for the principal Western European countries. The public investment priorities and claims mentioned above can be expected to raise the Japanese public expenditure proportion closer to that of the United States.

Although these changes will take time, and are likely to ensue whether the formal political leadership of the Japanese government is vested in the LDP or the JSP, the enhancement of JSP influence and leverage, whether exercised directly or indirectly, is likely to accelerate them. The result will be to reduce if not eliminate the structural imbalances that have characterized Japan's mercantilist economy, by lowering savings and raising domestic investment, thereby reducing the excess of domestic savings over investment; by reducing Japan's export surplus; and by reducing the disparity between domestic and foreign prices. The beneficiaries of these accelerated changes will be Japanese consumers and, perhaps inadvertently, Japan's trading partners through a more open, balanced, and competitive global economy.

Paradoxically, a bit of socialism in Japan can further capitalism in the United States and elsewhere.

Postaudit

Japan's Socialist Party did not win control of the Diet, but it did increase its representation (by 53 seats) and its national voting strength (by 7 percent), thereby acquiring one-half the number of seats held by the Liberal Democratic Party. Its increased influence seems more likely to take the form of LDP preemption of some of the JSP themes, as conjectured in the article's opening paragraph. And the downstream effects on the Japanese economy will probably turn out to be cloudy, congruent with those envisaged in the article.

47

The Coming Conflict in International Capital Markets

As the danger of global military conflict recedes, a different sort of global conflict seems likely to emerge in the 1990s. Its venue will be the international capital markets, and its causes and sources will result from a combination of circumstances: a substantial contraction of capital exports from the principal 1980s capital suppliers—Japan and Germany; and the increasing demands for capital imports in Eastern Europe and perhaps the Soviet Union, in conflict with Third World claimants in Latin America, South and Southeast Asia, Africa, and China.

These changes may be partly offset by other developments tending to increase capital supplies. But the offsets will be insufficient to reverse the larger and stronger forces tending toward contraction.

The likely result is that world capital markets will become increasingly tight and competitive. Most potential capital importers— in Latin America, Africa, South and Southeast Asia, and China—will face tighter capital supplies, higher real interest rates, and higher expected profit and dividend rates on the direct foreign and portfolio investment they seek to attract. And the burden of financing internal investment will tend increasingly to fall on their own domestic savings and on constraining domestic consumption.

In the second half of the 1980s, Japan and West Germany were the principal sources of global capital supplies. From 1987 to 1990, Japan and Germany had aggregate current account surpluses of about $250 and $180 billion, respectively, representing annual sources of international capital of over $80 and $60 billion, respectively. During the first half of the 1990s, these surpluses are likely to drop

A slightly abbreviated version of this essay was published by the New York Times *under the title "The Conflict of the 90s: Scarce Capital" on July 15, 1990.*

significantly. Those of Japan will probably fall under the combined effects of rising consumption propensities among the Japanese middle class and youth, an increasing proportion of the population who are aged (and hence tend to be nonsavers), growing government spending for public works and social welfare, and somewhat slower rates of growth in the economy as a whole. As an indication of this prospect, Japan's original estimate of its 1990 current account surplus with the United States of $49 billion has recently been reduced by one third, and an earlier estimate of its total global current account surplus has been lowered by about 25 percent. Even if Japan heeds the advice of a recent Ministry of Finance panel report recommending that a current account surplus should be maintained, its future size will probably decrease considerably.

The current account surpluses of Germany are also likely to decline, probably even more sharply than those of Japan, as a result of the immediate effects of unification. West Germany's decision to convert East German wages and pensions, as well as holdings of less than 4,000 ostmarks (about $2,370) to deutschmarks at a one-to-one rate (the black market rate between the ostmark and the deutschmark has been six or seven to one!), will preempt for East German consumption a substantial portion of West Germany's recent current account surpluses. And for the next few years at least, much of the remainder will probably be absorbed by efforts to increase public investment to reverse the extraordinary deterioration of East Germany's infrastructure—railroads, roads, bridges, communications, and the environment.

Indeed, one of the most remarkable results of glasnost in East Germany—a Socialist system that was reputed, until the second half of 1989, to have worked effectively—has been the revelation of the extent of deterioration in East Germany's capital stock. Prior to East German glasnost, estimates by the CIA and the World Bank placed East Germany's per-capita GNP in 1987 at 89 percent of that of West Germany! That these estimates were remarkably far from reality has become evident in the past year. Recent evidence suggests, for example, that East German consumption levels are far below those of West Germany, and that repairing and modernizing East Germany's industrial and infrastructure capital stocks would require about $180 and $118 billion, respectively, to raise them to West German levels.

The result is that Germany's capital exports will be significantly reduced by the large emerging claims accompanying unification.

What about possible offsets to these indications of tightened capital supplies from Japan and Germany? One possibility is that some of the "maturing" newly industrialized economies (NIEs), South Korea and Taiwan, may increase their net national savings and capital exports. But these increases will be well below the diminished surpluses of Japan and Germany. A potentially larger, but even more uncertain, offset may result from an upturn in the U.S. gross savings rate. The large increases that are expected in Social Security surpluses projected for the 1990s will be one contributing factor. Reductions in the federal budget deficit may also help, more assuredly if the reductions result from decreased government spending on goods and services than from tax increases (the latter may simply be paid by decreased personal and business savings rather than decreased consumption). Potential reductions in defense spending in the United States and elsewhere may also tend to increase global savings and contribute to increased world capital supplies.

Not surprisingly, the outlook is less than crystal clear. In a best-case scenario, the offsets may equal or even exceed the sharp reductions in the principal sources of the 1980s international capital supplies. In a more likely scenario, let alone a worst-case one, the forces that portend more severe constraints on global capital supplies will be stronger, as well as more probable, than the forces tending in the opposite direction.

The prospective contraction of global capital supplies foreshadows increasingly severe competition for these scarce resources among potential capital importers. To the extent that the policies of OECD governments consign part of the reduced capital supplies to certain politically critical regions and countries (notably Eastern Europe and possibly the Soviet Union), thereby fencing them off from the global capital market, the situation facing the Third World as a whole, and the next wave of "newly industrializing economies" in particular, will become even more tightly constrained.

In sum, the outlook in international capital markets in the first half of the 1990s is for higher returns on direct and portfolio foreign investment, and more exacting terms for sovereign debt in the absence of special political preferment. Such new institutions as the emerging development bank for Eastern Europe (and perhaps the Soviet Union) will exercise such special claims on already constrained international capital supplies. These special claims will increasingly be exercised at the expense of capital imports in most of the Third World.

Index

Selected List of RAND Books

Alexiev, Alexander R., and S. Enders Wimbush (eds). *Ethnic Minorities in the Red Army: Asset or Liability?* 1988.

Builder, Carl H. *The Masks of War: American Military Styles in Strategy and Analysis.* 1989.

Chassin, Mark R., et al. *The Appropriateness of Selected Medical and Surgical Procedures: Relationships to Geographical Variations.* 1989.

Dorfman, Robert, Paul A. Samuelson, and Robert M. Solow. *Linear Programming and Economic Analysis.* 1958; 1987.

Fainsod, Merle. *Smolensk under Soviet Rule.* 1958; 1989.

Gustafson, Thane. *Crisis Amid Plenty: The Politics of Oil and Gas and the Evolution of Energy Policy in the Soviet Union Since 1917.* 1989.

Horelick, Arnold L. (ed.). *U.S.-Soviet Relations: The Next Phase.* 1986.

Hosmer, Stephen T. *Constraints on U.S. Strategy in Third World Conflicts.* 1987.

Kanouse, David E., et al. *Changing Medical Practice through Technology Assessment: An Evaluation of the NIH Consensus Development Program.* 1989.

Klahr, Philip, and Donald A. Waterman (eds.). *Expert Systems: Techniques, Tools, and Applications.* 1986.

Korbonski, Andrzej, and Francis Fukuyama (eds.). *The Soviet Union and the Third World: The Last Three Decades.* 1987.

Leites, Nathan. *Soviet Style in Management.* 1985.

Leites, Nathan. *Soviet Style in War.* 1982.

Levine, Robert A. *Still the Arms Debate.* 1989.

Morrison, Peter A. (ed.). *A Taste of the Country: A Collection of Calvin Beale's Writings.* 1990.

Nerlich, Uwe, and James A. Thomson (eds.). *Conventional Arms Control and the Security of Europe.* 1988.

Nerlich, Uwe, and James A. Thomson (eds.). *The Soviet Problem in American-German Relations.* 1985.

Quade, Edward S., revised by Grace M. Carter. *Analysis for Public Decisions* (3rd ed.). 1989.

Ross, Randy L. *Government and the Private Sector: Who Should Do What?* 1988.

Williams, J.D. *The Compleat Strategyst: Being a Primer on the Theory of Games of Strategy.* 1954; 1966; 1986.

Wolf, Charles, Jr. *Foreign Aid: Theory and Practice in Southern Asia.* 1960.

Wolf, Charles, Jr. *Markets or Governments: Choosing between Imperfect Alternatives.* 1988.

Wolf, Charles, Jr., and Katharine Watkins Webb (eds.). *Developing Cooperative Forces in the Third World.* 1987.